Hiragana chart

MW01410146

n	d	t	z(j)	s	g	k		
な	だ	た	ざ	さ	が	か	あ	a
に	(ぢ) ji	ち chi	じ ji	し shi	ぎ	き	い	i
ぬ	づ zu	つ tsu	ず	す	ぐ	く	う	u
ね	で	て	ぜ	せ	げ	け	え	e
の	ど	と	ぞ	そ	ご	こ	お	o
にゃ nya		ちゃ cha	じゃ ja	しゃ sha	ぎゃ gya	きゃ kya		
にゅ nyu		ちゅ chu	じゅ ju	しゅ shu	ぎゅ gyu	きゅ kyu		
にょ nyo		ちょ cho	じょ jo	しょ sho	ぎょ gyo	きょ kyo		

Authors' acknowledgements

Special thanks are due to the following people who have made valuable contributions to the Course Book and the CDs.

Ken Hutchinson, Head of Asian Languages at Brisbane Grammar School, for writing much of the 'Japanese Writing' section and for other assistance; Yukari Irie and her family, and Shingo Adachi and his family, for generously providing us with many of the photos used in the 'Setsumei Koonaa' and 'Nani? Nani?' sections; Saburo Kobayashi of Seifu Gakuen for encouragement and assistance; Masato Kobayashi for generously writing and recording the three songs used in the book; Bill Twyman for writing and recording the introductory music, the Tensei music and the chord used to separate items on the CDs; John Rix of the Recording Studio Albion for patiently recording and editing the CDs; Shinichi Horiguchi and family for supplying photos; Itsuko Kitagawa, Jennie Brownlie-Smith and Karen Nishimura of the Queensland LOTE Centre for encouragement, advice and photos; Sally Shimada and Yuko Fujimitsu, Japanese Consultants of the New South Wales Department of Education and Training, and Yoshiko Furukawa, Chief Advisory Lecturer, The Japan Foundation, Sydney Language Centre, for their advice and assistance; Bronwyn Dewar of Brisbane State High School for advice and encouragement; Kyoto Meitoku School and Kansai Daigaku for permission to reproduce their photographs; Emma Minehan, Ken Minehan, Kaori Karino, Katsuhiko Kinoshita, Yasuhisa Watanabe, Taku Onishi and Sanshiro Ishida for enthusiastically rehearsing and reading on the CDs; and all others who have helped with this production.

mirai

JAPANESE COURSE BOOK

STAGE 1

MEG EVANS
YOKO MASANO
SETSUKO TANIGUCHI

Longman

Sydney, Melbourne, Brisbane, Perth and
associated companies around the world

Pearson Education Australia Pty Limited
95 Coventry Street
South Melbourne 3205 Australia

Offices in Sydney, Brisbane and Perth, and associated companies throughout the world.

First published 1999
Reprinted 2000, 2001 (twice)

Cover and text designed by Leigh Ashforth @ watershed art & design
Illustrated by Kate Ashforth, Paul Könye, Dimitrios Prokopis and Boris Silvestri
Cover illustration by Dimitrios Prokopis
Set in 12pt Goudy
Produced by Pearson Education Australia Pty Limited
Printed in Australia by the australian book connection

National Library of Australia
Cataloguing-in-Publication data

Evans, Meg, 1935– .
Mirai Japanese. Stage 1.

ISBN 0 7339 0425 4 (coursebook).
ISBN 0 7339 0482 3 (activity book).
ISBN 0 7339 0525 0 (compact disc).
ISBN 0 7339 0504 8 (teacher's book).

1. Japanese language – Textbooks for foreign speakers – English. 2. Japanese language – Problems, exercises, etc. I. Masano, Yoko. II. Taniguchi, Setsuko.

495.682421

Contents

PART 3 スポーツ と レジャー

Sport and leisure

LOTE – National Profile Correlation Grids

The following grids are an interpretation of the national profiles and can be used as a course outline. The references on the grids are to page numbers in the Course Book (CB); the Activity Book (AB); and the Teacher's Book (TB). The Aesthetic strand mentioned in the national profiles is taken to mean imaginative and creative learning experiences. Suggestions for these will be found mainly in the Teacher's Book.

Part 1 Unit 1	Content:	Proposed time span:
どうぞ　よろしく	Introductions, greetings	3–4 weeks

Main linguistic elements	
	Subject pronouns わたし、ぼく Titles せんせい、さん、くん Hiragana わ、た、し、は、ぼ、く、で、す
	Particle は Sentence patterns A は B です

Objectives

Learners can
- introduce themselves
- understand introductions
- introduce others
- use appropriate greetings
- read and write わたし、ぼく、です

Cultural awareness
- Japanese writing
- Japan/Australia
- polite titles
- bowing
- body language
- time of daily greetings
- things Japanese

Strands	Learning activities	Strand organisers: Interpersonal	Informational	Imaginative/creative	Script	Activities (multilevel strategies): できますか 1	ききましょう	かいわ	ゲーム	できますか 2	Summary わかった	Hiragana	ワードパズル	よみかきのれんしゅう	Extension activities	まんが	Self-assessment
Listening and speaking	introducing self to class	●													CB 15		
	understanding others' introductions	●				CB 2–3											
	role play			●		CB 6											
	identifying greetings from taped material	●							CB 14	CB 13					AB 5		
	playing language games	●															
	responding to taped material	●					AB 4								TB 3–4	CB 18	CB 19
	singing a greeting song	●															
Reading	reading a story dialogue		●														
	reading greetings		●														
	reading labelled photographs	●															
	playing hiragana games				●												
	completing puzzles				●												
	reading a manga	●															
Writing	copying hiragana syllables				●							CB 17					
	copying words written in hiragana				●								AB 9		TB 5, 6		
	writing an identification card for self and alien			●								AB 5–7		AB 8			
	writing a manga			●													

Cultural awareness (Listening and speaking):
- CB xxiii–xxix
- CB xxixi
- CB 4
- CB 9
- CB 10
- CB 12
- AB 1–3
- TB 5

Activities (Reading):

• story dialogue	CB 2–3
• greetings	CB 11
• なに？　なに？	CB 8
• game	CB 14
• song おはよう　みなさん	CB 15
• manga (extension)	CB 18
• hiragana	CB 16–17
• hidden hiragana	AB 6
• word puzzles	AB 9
• summary (わかった)	CB 7, 15

Part 1 Unit 2 なんさい ですか	Content: Personal information, numbers	Proposed time span: 3–4 weeks

Main linguistic elements	
	Counting 1–50 Age さい Questions なんさい ですか。でんわ ばんごうは なんばん ですか。 Hiragana さ、い、ん、ば、こ、ご、う、も Particle も Sentence patterns A も B です

Strands	Objectives	Strand organisers: Interpersonal	Informational	Imaginative/creative	Script	Activities (multilevel strategies): できますか 1	ききましょう	かいわ	ゲーム	できますか 2	Summary わかった	Hiragana	ワードパズル	よみかきのれんしゅう	Extension activities	まんが	Self-assessment	Cultural awareness
	Learners can • count to 50 • say and understand ages, phone numbers • read and write 〜さい です。 でんわ ばんごうは … です。																	• counting systems • unlucky numbers • family names • kanji numbers • Teru teru bozu
Listening and speaking	Learning activities																	
	• counting games	●				CB 20–21		AB 11							TB 19–23			• CB 22, 30
	• drawing pictures from co-ordinates			●			AB 10											• CB 28 • CB 29
	• form filling		●							CB 31								• CB 26
	• listening activities related to understanding phone numbers, ages		●			CB 25												
	• playing number games	●							CB 32									
	• participating in imaginative role plays			●				AB 11								CB 36	CB 37	

Reading: learning activities	Interpersonal	Informational	Imaginative/creative	Script	Activities	
• reading a story dialogue		●			• story dialogue	CB 20–21
• recognising syllables, words and phrases				●	• かぞえましょう	CB 23
					• なに？ なに？	CB 33
• recognising kanji numbers				●	• game	CB 32
• completing word puzzles	●				• manga (extension)	CB 36
• choosing a penfriend		●			• hiragana	CB 34–35
• reading a manga		●			• hidden hiragana	AB 13
					• hiragana and kanji puzzles	AB 17–18
					• summary (わかった)	CB 26, 33
					• kanji numbers (extension)	CB 29

Writing: learning activities	Interpersonal	Informational	Imaginative/creative	Script	Hiragana	ワードパズル	よみかきのれんしゅう	Extension activities
• writing hiragana syllables				●				
• reproducing words and sentences written in hiragana and kanji numbers				●	AB 12–14			
• completing sentences		●			CB 35			AB 16–17
• completing puzzles			●			AB 18	AB 15	
• writing an imaginative message and manga	●							

Part 1 Unit 3 どこに　すんで　いますか

Content: Residence, nationality, more greetings

Proposed time span: 3–4 weeks

Main linguistic elements

Particle に
Sentence pattern *Place* に　すんでいます。
～じん　です。
Idiom ああ、そう　ですか。

Questions どこに　すんでいますか。
おくには　どこ　ですか。
Hiragana に、ま、じ、せ、と、ど、な、か
Further aisatsu in the home.

Objectives

Learners can
- ask and say where they live
- ask and say nationality
- understand and use greetings in the home

Cultural awareness
- Japanese towns and villages
- Oshogatsu, Obon
- greetings in the home

Strands	Learning activities	Interpersonal	Informational	Imaginative/creative	Script	できますか 1	ききましょう	かいわ	ゲーム	できますか 2	Summary わかった	Hiragana	ワードパズル	よみかきのれんしゅう	Extension activities	まんが	Self-assessment	Cultural awareness
Listening and speaking	• producing words, phrases and sentences related to saying where they live and nationality	●				CB 38–39			CB 43	CB 51					TB 31–33, 36 AB 19	CB 55		• CB 46–47 • CB 48 • CB 49 • TB 35
	• participating in activities involving listening and responding to taped exercises		●			CB 42	AB 19	AB 20										
	• playing games	●															CB 55	
	• participating in role plays		●															
Reading	• reading personal information		●															
	• recognition of syllables, words and phrases			●														
	• reading a dialogue aloud				●													
	• doing word puzzles and crosswords	●																
	• reading a form		●															
	• reading a manga		●															
Writing	• reproducing hiragana				●							CB 54						
	• reproducing words and sentences				●													
	• completing puzzles	●										AB 21, 23	AB 26–27			AB 25		
	• filling in a conversation		●															
	• filling in missing syllables	●												AB 24				
	• completing a form		●															
	• writing a manga			●														

Reading activities (multilevel strategies):

- story dialogue CB 38–39
- map どこに　すんでいますか CB 44
- なに？　なに？ CB 52
- game CB 43
- manga (extension) CB 54
- hiragana CB 53–4
- hidden hiragana AB 22
- forms AB 24
- puzzles AB 26–27
- summary (わかった) CB 45, 52

Part 2 Unit 4 なん ねんせい ですか	Content: School grades, timetables, subjects	Proposed time span: 3–4 weeks

Main linguistic elements	
grades 〜ねんせい です periods 〜じかんめ です Questions なんねんせい ですか。 すきな かもくは なん ですか。	Particle と Sentence patterns すうがくは 1じかんめと 2じかんめ です。 すきな かもくは〜です Hiragana き、ぎ、ね、え、お、り、れ

Objectives

Learners can
- ask and say their school grade
- ask and say what period the various subjects are
- ask and say what their favourite subjects are

Strands	Learning activities	Interpersonal	Informational	Aesthetic	Script	できますか 1	ききましょう	かいわ	ゲーム	できますか 2	Summary わかった	Hiragana	ワードパズル	よみかきのれんしゅう	Extension activities	まんが	Self-assessment	Cultural awareness
		Strand organisers				Activities (multilevel strategies)												• school system in Japan • comparable grades • school life in Japan • origami ☆
Listening and speaking	• producing words and phrases related to school grades and subjects	●				CB 58–59			CB 64	CB 68–					TB 48	CB 76		• CB 64 • CB 66 • CB 71
	• participating in activities involving listening and responding to taped exercises		●	☆		CB 70	AB 28	AB 30							AB 29			
	• playing games, bingo	●																
	• participating in role play related to school grades and timetables		●														CB 77	
Reading	• reading and understanding information about grades and subjects	●				• story dialogue CB 58–59 • にほんの かもく CB 61 • what class do they belong to? CB 62 • なに？ なに？ CB 70 • reading a letter AB 36 • game CB 63 • manga (extension) CB 74 • hiragana CB 72 • hiragana mozaic AB 32 • hiragana puzzles AB 38 • summary (わかった) CB 65, 71 TB 48												
	• recognition of syllables words and phrases				●													
	• reading captions			●														
	• doing word puzzles	●																
	• reading and explaining a letter		●															
	• reading a manga				●													
Writing	• reproducing hiragana syllables				●							CB 75			TB 49	AB 37		
	• reproducing words and sentences written in hiragana				●													
	• completing a conversation		●									AB 31	AB 38					
	• filling in a timetable	●										33, 34		AB 35–36				
	• completing puzzles	●																
	• writing a manga			●														

Part 2 Unit 5 りかは おもしろい です	Content: Describing subjects, teachers, lunches	Proposed time span: 3–4 weeks

Main linguistic elements		
	Adjectives Particles よ、の Questions A は adjective ですか。 Expressions はい、どうぞ。〜は ちょっと	Sentence patterns A は adjective ですよ。 ぼくの／わたしの すきな たべものは 〜 です。 Sentence 1 でも sentence 2 Hiragana の、ろ、や、つ、ら、あ、よ、む

Strands	Objectives Learners can • ask and give opinions about subjects, teachers and food • offer and decline food	Strand organisers: Interpersonal	Informational	Aesthetic	Script	Activities (multilevel strategies): できますか 1	ききましょう	かいわ	ゲーム	できますか 2	Summary わかった	Hiragana	ワードパズル	よみかきのれんしゅう	Extension activities	まんが	Self-assessment	Cultural awareness • School club activities • School lunches • Fukuwarai
Listening and speaking	Learning activities																	
	• producing words and phrases and sentences related to describing subjects, teachers and food	●				CB 78–79 CB 83	AB 39	AB 40	CB 92	CB 91					AB 39 TB 60 65 66 68	CB 96		• CB 84 • CB 85 • CB 83 • TB 62
	• participating in activities involving listening and responding to taped exercises		●															
	• playing games, bingo		●														CB 97	
	• participating in role plays	●																
Reading	• reading and understanding information about school subjects, teachers and food. Recognition of syllables, words and sentences		●			• story dialogue • adjective chart • game • なに？ なに？ • manga (extension) • hiragana • hiragana mozaic • Naoko's faxes • puzzles • summary (わかった)						CB 78–79 CB 78 CB 90 CB 91 CB 94 CB 92 AB 42 AB 46 AB 48 CB 83, 91						
	• reading a dialogue aloud	●																
	• completing puzzles	●																
	• reading faxes		●															
	• reading a manga				●													
Writing	• reproducing hiragana syllables, words and sentences				●							CB 95 AB 41, 43	AB 47 48	AB 46	TB 61	AB 45		
	• answering questions				●													
	• filling in word puzzles		●															
	• filling in a conversation	●																
	• writing a manga	●																
	• writing a timetable			●														
	• labelling		●		●													

Part 2 Unit 6 せんせい みて ください

Content: Classroom objects, commands, requests, encouragement

Proposed time span: 4–5 weeks

Main linguistic elements

Requests 〜て ください。〜を 〜て ください。もう いちど 〜 ください。 Particle を、ね
Permission 〜 ても いい ですか。〜を 〜ても いい ですか。はい、いいです。いいえ、だめ です。
Expressions あのう。できました。がんばって。どう いたしまして。
Hiragana み、け、げ、を、ず、た、だ、ち、ふ、ぶ、ひ、ぴ

Strands — Objectives

Learners can
- make requests
- ask for, grant and deny permission
- say they have finished
- understand encouragement
- read and write requests and the names of classroom objects

Cultural awareness
- brush writing (shodō)
- The Tale of Genji
- origin of the name 日本
- Shinto
- Amaterasu

Strand	Learning activities	Interpersonal	Informational	Aesthetic	Script	できますか 1	ききましょう	かいわ	ゲーム	できますか 2	Summary わかった	Hiragana	ワードパズル	よみかきのれんしゅう	Extension activities	まんが	Self-assessment	Cultural awareness
Listening and speaking	producing words and phrases related to the classroom and classroom talk	●				CB 98–99			CB 113	CB 111					TB 78, 79, 82, 83	CB 117		• CB 105 • CB 106 • TB 82
	participating in activities involving listening to and responding to taped exercises		●			CB 102	AB 49	AB 50							AB 49			
	playing games	●																
	participating in role plays		●														CB 118	
	singing a song	●		●														
Reading	recognition of syllables, words and sentences				●	• story dialogue CB 98–99 • labelling CB 102 • なに？ なに？ CB 104 • game CB 113 • manga (extension) CB 117 • hiragana CB 115 • hidden hiragana AB 15 • hiragana puzzles AB 56–58												
	reading and understanding classroom requests		●															
	reading dialogues and understanding them			●														
	playing bingo	●																
	doing word puzzles			●														
	reading a manga	●																
Writing	reproducing hiragana syllables, words and sentences				●								AB 57–58 CB 116					
	labelling classroom items				●									AB 54 55				
	filling in speech bubbles		●															
	designing a manga			●								AB 51, 53				AB 56		
	completing puzzles	●													TB 80			

Part 3 Unit 7 しあいは 8じに はじまります	**Content:** Daily events, time, hours and minutes	**Proposed time span:** 3–5 weeks

Main linguistic elements	Questions いま なんじ ですか、なんじに 〜を しますか。 Particles に、と Sentence patterns ひろくんは 7 じに おきます。 いぬと あそびます。〜を します。 Adjectives おそい ですね。はやい ですね。 Hiragana る、び、ふ、ぶ、へ、ね、そ、ぞ、こ、ご

Strands	Objectives	Strand organisers: Interpersonal	Strand organisers: Informational	Strand organisers: Aesthetic	Strand organisers: Script	Activities (multilevel strategies): できますか 1	ききましょう	かいわ	ゲーム	できますか 2	Summary わかった	Hiragana	ワードパズル	よみかきのれんしゅう	Extension activities	まんが	Self-assessment	Cultural awareness
	Learners can • ask and give the time • say what time they do things • understand other's schedules • read and write what time they and others do things																	• popular Western sports • traditional sports: sumo, kendo, judo, karate • hiragana face
Listening and speaking	**Learning activities**																	
	• producing phrases and sentences related to asking and telling the time, saying what time they do things and with whom	●	●			CB 120–121 CB 125	AB 59	AB 61	CB 126	CB 134 135					TB 97, 98 AB 60	CB 140		• CB 128 • CB 129 • CB 136 • TB 99
	• participating in activities involving listening and responding to taped exercises		●															
	• choosing a room-mate			●													CB 141	
	• participating in role plays			●														
Reading	• reading and understanding information about time, daily activities, leisure activities	●	●			• story dialogue CB 120–121 • clock chart CB 124 • game CB 126 • daily schedules CB 130–131 • なに？ なに？ CB 137 • manga (extension) CB 140 • hiragana CB 138–139 • essay AB 65 • puzzles AB 67 • summary (わかった) CB 127, 136 TB 101												
	• recognition of syllables, words and sentences				●													
	• reading a dialogue aloud		●															
	• completing puzzles	●																
	• reading an essay		●															
	• reading a manga		●															
Writing	• reproducing hiragana syllables, words and sentences				●							CB 139						
	• answering questions	●			●													
	• filling in word puzzles		●															
	• filling in speech bubbles		●									AB 62–63	AB 67–68	AB 64	TB 99, 100	AB 66		
	• completing sentences		●															
	• writing a schedule			●														

Part 3 Unit 8 どこへ いきますか

Content: Places to go to, things to do

Proposed time span: 3–5 weeks

Main linguistic elements

Questions どこへ／に いきますか。
だれと いきますか。
だれと うみに いきますか。

Particle へ

Sentence patterns Place へ／に いきます。
Person と place へ いきます。
いっしょに へ／を ～ましょう。

Hiragana ゆ、きゃ、きゅ、きょ、しゃ、しゅ、しょ、ちゃ、ちゅ、ちょ

Strands	Objectives	Strand organisers				Activities (multilevel strategies)												Cultural awareness
	Learners can • ask and say where they are going • ask and say with whom they are going • understand other's intentions • issue invitations • read and write what they can say	Interpersonal	Informational	Aesthetic	Script	できますか 1	ききましょう	かいわ	ゲーム	できますか 2	Summary わかった	Hiragana	ワードパズル	よみかきのれんしゅう	Extension activities	まんが	Self-assessment	• origin of kanji • oracle bones • school execursions in Japan • Setsubun, Mamemaki and Oni
	Learning activities																	
Listening and speaking	• producing phrases and sentences related to going places, saying who is going with them; issuing invitations	●				CB 142–143			CB 155	CB 154					TB 117, 118	CB 162		• CB 149 • CB 158 • CB 156 • TB 115
	• participating in activities involving listening and responding to audio material		●			CB 146	AB 69	AB 70										
	• playing games	●	●															
	• participating in role plays		●	●													CB 162	
Reading	• recognition of syllables, words and phrases	●																
	• reading and understanding sentences related to going places	●		●														
	• reading dialogues	●																
	• completing puzzles	●																
	• reading a manga		●															
	• reading messages		●															
	• reading a letter	●																
Writing	• reproducing hiragana syllables				●							CB 160 AB 71–72 AB 75–76	AB 73–74, 79–80	AB 74, 77	TB 119	AB 78		
	• reproducing words and sentences				●													
	• writing a reply to messages, a letter		●															
	• filling in speech bubbles	●																
	• designing a manga	●		●														
	• completing puzzles	●																

Reading activities:

Activity	Reference
• story dialogue	CB 142–43
• どこへ いきますか。	CB 147
• ぶんかさい	CB 150
• なに？ なに？	CB 157
• game	CB 155
• manga (extension)	CB 162
• hiragana	CB 159–160
• hiragana puzzles	AB 73
• messages	AB 77
• summary（わかった）	CB 148, 156

Part 3 Unit 9 ひこうきで　いきましょう	Content: Leisure time in the past, transport	Proposed time span: 3–5 weeks

Main linguistic elements

Questions どこへ　いきましたか。なんで　いきます(ました)か。　Particle で
きのう　なんようび　でしたか。なんようびに　いきます(ました)か。
Sentence patterns きのう　まちへ　いきました。きのう　おんがくを　ききました。
Days of the week

Strands	Objectives	Strand organisers: Interpersonal	Informational	Aesthetic	Script	Activities (multilevel strategies): できますか 1	ききましょう	かいわ	ゲーム	できますか 2	Summary わかった	Hiragana	ワードパズル	よみかきのれんしゅう	Extension activities	まんが	Self-assessment	Cultural awareness
	Learners can • ask and understand where someone went • ask and understand modes of transport • ask and understand days of the week • read and write what they can say																	• train system in Japan • origin of days of the week • origami
Listening and speaking	**Learning activities** • asking about and saying what they did, what day they do/did things: what transport they used	●				CB 164/165 CB 169	AB 81–82	AB 83	CB 176	CB 175					TB 133, 134, 135 AB 81	CB 180		• CB 171 • CB 172 • CB 170 • TB 137
	• participating in activities involving listening to taped exercises		●															
	• filling in a school timetable		●															
	• participating in role plays		●	●													CB 181	
	• singing a song			●	●													
Reading	• recognition of words and sentences and kanji				●	• story dialogue CB 164/165 • なんで　がっこうへ　いきますか CB 168 • game CB 176 • なに？　なに？ CB 178 • manga (extension) CB 180 • hiragana CB 179 • puzzles AB 89–91 • read a dialy AB 86 • summary (わかった) CB 170, 177												
	• reading and understanding information about past activities and transport used		●		●													
	• reading a dialogue aloud	●	●															
	• completing puzzles		●															
	• reading a diary			●														
Writing	• reproducing kanji for days of the week				●										CB 179			
	• reproducing sentences				●													
	• writing a self-introduction	●										AB 85						
	• filling in word puzzles	●											AB 89–91	AB 86 87	TB 136 AB 84–85	AB 88		
	• filling in speech bubbles		●															
	• writing a dialogue		●															
	• writing a diary			●														

Introduction

Konnichi wa! Welcome to Mirai Stage 1.

You are about to start learning Japanese. Soon you will be able to talk about yourself and understand what other people are saying about themselves. You will also learn to read and write the Japanese syllabary called hiragana and a few of the picture writing called kanji.

You will meet the following people who attend a judō academy run by Mr Tanaka. Mr Tanaka is a famous judō expert who now lives in Australia. He encourages all the students who attend his academy to speak in Japanese, because they are all learning Japanese at school.

Tanaka-sensei

Karen Scott

Johnny Lee

Naomi Akimoto

Hiro Yamaguchi

Ken Thomson

Masashi Yamada

Nicki Fenwick

You will also meet Yukari and Shingo, real Japanese teenagers who are there to help you and to tell you about their lives in Japan.

Hi! I'm Yukari. I'm in grade 8. Shingo and I will explain any new expressions.

Hi! I'm Shingo. I'm in grade 10.

You will also meet the Ninja, a historical character from feudal Japan. He will help you in lots of ways.

The ninja were members of the secret service in feudal times. They were trained from childhood in martial arts. They were not only highly skilled fighters but also developed high powers of concentration that enabled them to withstand pain and bodily discomfort. They were able to enter the castles of their masters' enemies without being seen and find out the enemies' secret plans. Unlike modern spies, who can use cameras and tape recorders, the ninja had to memorise everything.

The ninja were so skilful, people thought that they had magic powers. They did not have magic powers but they did have:

- discipline
- determination
- daring.

Discipline was needed to keep practising their martial arts every day, so that they were constantly becoming faster. Their reflexes were almost instantaneous. **Determination** was necessary to keep their goals in sight and **daring** gave them the courage to try anything.

These attributes will help you too succeed in learning a new language. That is why we have chosen the Ninja as your guide and inspiration.

Finding your way around this Course Book

The first section, called **Japanese writing**, is an explanation of the way in which Japanese is written. It is a good idea to read it before you start so that you have some understanding of Japanese writing. You do not need to remember everything; just use it for reference as you learn to write hiragana.

The rest of the book is divided into three parts, with three units in each part. Within the units you will find the following icons.

This means that the section is on compact disc.

This indicates a pair-work activity in which you take turns to play the characters. The characters are: **Kitsune**, a Japanese fox, and **Tanuki**, a Japanese raccoon dog.

Kitsune is famous in Japanese folklore because he is able to trick human beings as well as other animals. There are many folktales in which he changes himself into human shape, either male or female. In the myths and fables of Japan, Kitsune was also the messenger of Inari, the god of the rice fields.

Tanuki is also a character who frequently appears in Japanese folktales. He also likes to trick people and can take on human form. He is an amusing character who likes to do silly things. When these two come together they always try to trick each other.

AB p. 4

This is a reference to a page in the Activity Book, where you will find more activities related to what you have been learning.

せつめい コーナー
Explanation corner

Explanation corner. Here you will find explanations about new sentences and expressions.

Particles

Particles. The Ninja gives you special help here and in other sections.

できますか
Dekimasuka
CAN YOU DO IT?

Can you do it? These are activities to test your understanding.

わかった！
Wakatta!
I'VE GOT IT!

I've got it! These summaries show what you know.

インフォ
Info
DID YOU KNOW?

Did you know? These pages tell you interesting information about Japan.

べんきょうの　こつ

What's your secret? Handy study hints!

あそびましょう

Just for fun! Things that Japanese children learn to do.

ひらがな

Reading and writing hiragana. Practice in reading and writing.

てんせい

Tensei. A continuing manga about Tensei, an alien who visits Japan.

WHAT A USEFUL EXPRESSION!

What a useful expression! That's exactly what they are!

チェック　しましょう

Let's check! A vocabulary and checklist, where you can tick everything you have learned to do and mark your progress up Mt Fuji.

Japanese writing

Japanese is a language that does not use the alphabet to write sounds and words. In fact, Japanese writing consists of three types of writing. They are called, kanji, hiragana and katakana.

What are kanji?

The kanji system was brought to Japan from China more than 1500 years ago by visiting Buddhist priests and scholars. For a while, scholars in Japan wrote in Chinese—just like scholars in Europe and Britain wrote in Latin and Greek.

Kanji originally developed from the pictures of things. Indeed, there are still many kanji that actually look like the word they represent. For example, it is easy to see that 山 looks like a mountain—and that is exactly what it means!

Can you guess what these other kanji mean?

山
川
木
日

You often see picture-writing in English. Can you think of any other examples?

1800 555 999
Tom
Kelly
BRISBANE 4-DAY OUTLOOK

Of course there are many kanji that do not look like their original picture at all. This is because the picture has been simplified or changed over the centuries.

For example 上 is the kanji for *up*, and 下 is the kanji for *down*. Originally, they were written like this:

There are also many kanji that represent ideas, or things that cannot be drawn simply. They are formed from a combination of kanji or elements of kanji.

is a combination of the kanji for *mountain* 山 plus *up* 上 and *down* 下. It means *a mountain pass*.

Notice that in English we have to use twelve letters to express this idea, but in Japanese it can be expressed with one kanji.

In all, Japanese primary school children learn to read and write about 1000 kanji. By the end of high school, they should know how to read and write almost 2000. In this Course Book you will only learn a few easy kanji, which you should enjoy learning to read and write. Kanji are not like our alphabet; they are used to represent words and not to spell them out. So every time you learn a new kanji, you have to learn how to say it, or read it aloud.

When the Japanese tried to write Japanese using Chinese kanji, they found it rather inconvenient, because Japanese is quite different from Chinese. For example, they needed to write word endings that do not occur in Chinese. To give you an English example, the word *jump* could be written with a kanji but the different endings of the word, such as *jump<u>ing</u>*, or *jump<u>ed</u>* could not be written with kanji. They therefore developed kana, two different scripts that represent sounds. Every single word can be spelt using these scripts.

What are the other two kinds of writing for?

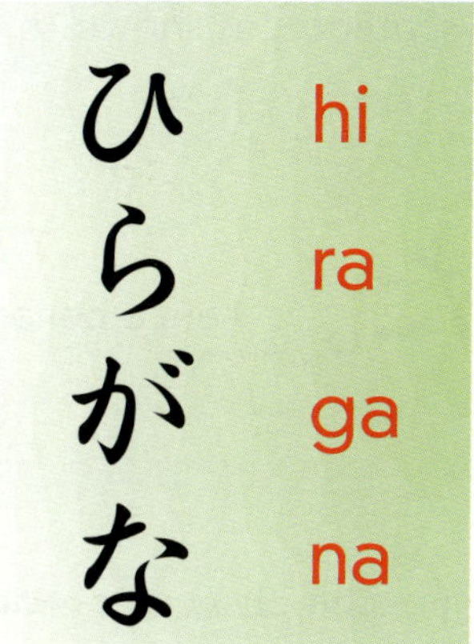
ひらがな
hi ra ga na

One of these two types of kana is **hiragana**. Hiragana is the first script that Japanese children learn. Using hiragana, you can write anything that you can say in Japanese. As soon as you have learned it, you can start to write to a penfriend in Japan. Hiragana is a form of writing that has forty-six symbols. Each symbol represents a syllable. That means that each hiragana symbol is used to write a *sound*. The hiragana symbols do not have any meaning by themselves. Hiragana can be used to write every single Japanese word by spelling it out. Hiragana symbols are mostly rounded in shape.

けいこさん，こんにちは。
AIR MAIL
MISS KEIKO AOKI
2-3-5 SHINBASHI
MINATO-KU
TOKYO
JAPAN 105-0001

カタカナ
ka ta ka na

Katakana is the name of the other type of kana. It also has forty-six symbols that are used to write the sounds that make up a word. They are exactly the same sounds as in hiragana but are written with straighter, sharper lines. Katakana is used to write foreign (mostly English) words that have been absorbed into the Japanese language. It is also used for emphasis or to give a special look to certain styles of writing, such as comics. Onomatopoeic words—like buzz, hiss and clatter—are also written in katakana.

メークアップアーチスト
Makeup artist
テレビ
Television
カメラ
Camera

All three scripts (kanji, hiragana and katakana) can be used in the same sentence, as shown in the following example.

私はバナナを食べました。
I ate a banana.
kanji hiragana katakana hiragana kanji hiragana

In this Course Book we will concentrate on learning hiragana as soon as possible. It makes good sense to learn hiragana first. This allows you to write and read full sentences even if you do not know any kanji.

The hiragana syllabary

Here are the forty-six basic hiragana symbols. All but six of the symbols stand for a syllable consisting of a consonant and a vowel. For example, *ka*, *ki*, *ku*, *ke*, *ko*. Syllables that do not consist of a vowel plus a consonant are the five vowel sounds *a*, *i*, *u*, *e*, *o* and the one consonant *n*. Roomaji (Japanese that is written using the Roman alphabet) has been placed underneath to help you. Your teacher will help you to learn how to pronounce each syllable.

Start here and read down.

11	10	9	8	7	6	5	4	3	2	1
ん n	わ wa	ら ra	や ya	ま ma	は ha	な na	た ta	さ sa	か ka	あ a
		り ri		み mi	ひ hi	に ni	ち chi	し shi	き ki	い i
		る ru	ゆ yu	む mu	ふ fu	ぬ nu	つ tsu	す su	く ku	う u
		れ re		め me	へ he	ね ne	て te	せ se	け ke	え e
	を o	ろ ro	よ yo	も mo	ほ ho	の no	と to	そ so	こ ko	お o

Dakuten (゛) and handakuten (゜)

These forty-six hiragana symbols are extended by the use of two signs. These are called **dakuten** (゛) and **handakuten** (゜).

Syllables that start with *g*, *z*, *j*, *d*, *b* and *p* are written by putting these special little marks to the top right of the sounds that start with *k*, *s*, *t* and *h*.

	6	5	4	3	2	1
ぱ pa	ば ba		だ da	ざ za	が ga	
ぴ pi	び bi		ぢ ji	じ ji	ぎ gi	
ぷ pu	ぶ bu		づ zu	ず zu	ぐ gu	
ぺ pe	べ be		で de	ぜ ze	げ ge	
ぽ po	ぼ bo		ど do	ぞ zo	ご go	

Other sounds

Some syllables are created by combining a normal-sized hiragana with a small-sized hiragana: や *ya*, ゆ *yu* or よ *yo*.

りゃ rya	みゃ mya	ひゃ hya	にゃ nya	ちゃ cha	しゃ sha	きゃ kya
りゅ ryu	みゅ myu	ひゅ hyu	にゅ nyu	ちゅ chu	しゅ shu	きゅ kyu
りょ ryo	みょ myo	ひょ hyo	にょ nyo	ちょ cho	しょ sho	きょ kyo

Once you have learned the hiragana symbols, it is fairly easy to write full Japanese words. You don't have to worry about learning lots of spelling (as you do in English), because hiragana is a phonetic syllabary and that means you write the words as they sound. For example, the word for Japan is *Nihon*, and you write it にほん.

Rules for writing words

Things you need to know

There are a few simple rules to remember when writing hiragana.

To double a consonant

You must put a small っ (tsu) before the consonant you wish to double.

For example, *itte* is written いって. Notice the position of the little っ.

This rule does not apply when you double an n sound. Instead you use hiragana ん.

For example: *minna* is written みんな.

To extend a vowel sound

Just write the relevant vowel after the syllable you wish to extend.

For example:

okaasan is written おかあさん

oniisan is written おにいさん

kuuki is written くうき

oneesan is written おねえさん.

The only exception to this rule is the *o* vowel, which is almost always extended using the *u* symbol.

For example, *otōsan* is written おとうさん.

In this Course Book, all *o* that are extended with a *u* symbol are written in roomaji with a line over the *o*, like this: *ō*. The few words that are extended using the *o* symbol will be written in roomaji with a double oo. For example, おおさか would be written Oosaka.

Particles

Your teacher will tell you about particles in Japanese. When you learn about them, you will need to know that three of them are written using different hiragana from the way they are pronounced.

The particle *wa* is written は.

The particle *e* is written へ.

The particle *o* is written を.

Punctuation

Full stops are written 。.
Commas are written 、.

Across or down the page?

ひめちゃん、たいせつに つかってね。
2がつごうから、
ひめちゃんが
いろいろな ひとに
へんしんして、かつやく
するよ。おたのしみにね。

Perhaps you have already noticed that Japanese can be written across the page, just like English, or down the page from right to left. Traditionally, Japanese was always written down the page, but in modern times the English way is commonly used. Magazines and newspapers use both ways of writing on the same page because it gives great scope for interesting designs.

By the way, when the combined syllables such as きゃ、きゅ、きょ are written down the page, the small syllable is placed below and to the right.

❶トーマスは、はたらくのが　だいすき。
とくに　きゃくしゃの　アニーと
クララベルを　ひっぱって　いる　ときが
いちばん　たのしいです。

Hiragana order

As you know, dictionaries and word lists in English are written in alphabetical order. Naturally, Japanese word lists and dictionaries are written in hiragana order. This order is the same order as the syllabary chart: a, i, u, e, o, ka, ki, ku, ke, ko and so on. The dictionary at the end of this Course Book is in hiragana order, but to help you get started, there is a list of the new vocabulary under topic headings at the end of each unit. Within the topics, the words are listed in hiragana order.

Roomaji

While you are learning hiragana, roomaji will be written under the Japanese script to help you. When a particle is written in roomaji a space has been placed between the word and the particle to help you to recognise that it is a particle and not part of the word. For example, *sensei wa* means *as for the teacher*. The word for teacher is *sensei* not *senseiwa*. The *wa* is a particle. A hyphen has been placed between words and suffixes for the same reason.

Also, Japanese is not normally written with spaces between the words. You will get used to this at a later stage, when you know some kanji. For now, though, you will find spaces between all the words.

There is a red overlay provided with this book. Use it when you are ready to read hiragana without help from the roomaji.

Australia's Japanese connections

AB pp. 1–3

Find your state's sister prefecture and your capital city's sister city and connect them on the map.

Victoria	Aichi Prefecture
Western Australia	Hyōgo Prefecture
New South Wales	Metropolitan Tōkyō
Queensland	Saitama Prefecture Oosaka Prefecture
South Australia	Okayama Prefecture
Melbourne	Oosaka
Hobart	Yaizu
Brisbane	Kōbe
Perth	Kagoshima
Sydney	Nagoya
Adelaide	Himeji

Hokkaidō Region
Sapporo
Tōhoku Region
AOMORI
Aomori
AKITA
Akita
IWATE
Morioka
YAMAGATA
Yamagata
MIYAGI
Sendai
FUKUSHIMA
Fukushima
Niigata
NIIGATA
Chuubu Region
ISHIKAWA
Kanazawa
TOYAMA
Toyama
TOCHIGI
Utsunomiya
GUNMA
Maebashi
Nagano
NAGANO
IBARAKI
Mito
SAITAMA
Urawa
TOKYO
Tokyo
Chiba
CHIBA
Kofu
YAMANASHI
Yokohama
KANAGAWA
Kantō Region
FUKUI
Fukui
GIFU
Gifu
Nagoya
AICHI
Shizuoka
SHIZUOKA
Chuugoku Region
TOTTORI
Tottori
Matsue
SHIMANE
OKAYAMA
Okayama
HYOGO
Kōbe
KYOTO
Kyōto
SHIGA
Otsu
Tsu
MIE
Osaka
OSAKA
Nara
NARA
Wakayama
WAKAYAMA
Kinki Region
HIROSHIMA
Hiroshima
YAMAGUCHI
Yamaguchi
KAGAWA
Takamatsu
Tokushima
TOKUSHIMA
Matsuyama
EHIME
Kōchi
KOCHI
Shikoku Region
FUKUOKA
Fukuoka
SAGA
Saga
OITA
Oita
NAGASAKI
Nagasaki
Kumamoto
KUMAMOTO
MIYAZAKI
Miyazaki
Kagoshima
KAGOSHIMA
Kyuushuu Region
Darwin
NORTHERN TERRITORY
QUEENSLAND
WESTERN AUSTRALIA
SOUTH AUSTRALIA
Brisbane
NEW SOUTH WALES
Perth
Adelaide
Sydney
VICTORIA
Melbourne
TASMANIA
Hobart

part 1

Tomodachi

ともだち

Getting to know you

At the end of Part 1 you will be able to:

- greet people at different times of the day
- introduce yourself and say your age
- tell someone your phone number and where you live
- understand others' self-introductions
- read and write self-introductions in hiragana.

You will also find out some interesting things about Japan.

Unit 1

どうぞ よろしく
Dōzo yoroshiku

How do you do?

1
TANAKA JUDO ACADEMY
2
3
せんせい、
Sensei,
こんにちは
konnichi wa.
ケンくん、
Ken-kun,
こんにちは。
konnichi wa.
4
こんにちは。
Konnichi wa.
こんにちは。おなまえは？
Konnichi wa. Onamae wa?
5
カレン です。どうぞ よろしく。
Karen desu. Dōzo yoroshiku.
JUDO LESSONS TIME TABLE
6
たなか です。どうぞ よろしく。
Tanaka desu. Dōzo yoroshiku.

7
みなさん。
Minasan.
JUDO
8
みなさん、カレンさん です。
Minasan, Karen-san desu.
9
わたしは ニッキー です。
Watashi wa Nikkii desu.
どうぞ よろしく。
Dōzo yoroshiku.
わたしは なおみ です。
Watashi wa Naomi desu.
どうぞ よろしく。
Dōzo yoroshiku.
10
ぼくは ひろ です。
Boku wa Hiro desu.
どうぞ よろしく。
Dōzo yoroshiku.
ぼくは ジョニー です。
Boku wa Jonii desu.
どうぞ よろしく。
Dōzo yoroshiku.

できますか
Dekimasuka
CAN YOU DO IT?

Can you find …

* three ways to address someone?
* a word that means *hello*?
* an expression that means *Pleased to meet you*?
* how to give your name?
* how to ask someone's name?
* a word that means *everyone*?

せつめい コーナー
Setsumei koonaa

Explanation corner

How do I introduce myself?

To introduce yourself, just say your name and add です **desu.** Then add どうぞ よろしく **Dōzo yoroshiku,** which means *Pleased to meet you.*

If I am with others who are introducing themselves I say ぼくは しんご です。**Boku wa Shingo desu.** This means *As for me I am Shingo.* Girls say わたしは **watashi wa** instead of ぼくは **boku wa.**

It is better to wait for someone to introduce themselves rather than asking for their names, but teachers and group leaders may ask for names by just saying おなまえは? **Onamae wa?**

KUN
SAN
SENSEI

We say くん **kun** after boys' names and さん **san** after girls' names. We also say さん **san** after adults' names and せんせい **sensei** after teachers' names. Got that?

Oh, by the way, we *never* say くん **kun**, さん **san** or せんせい **sensei** after our *own* names. Can you guess why?

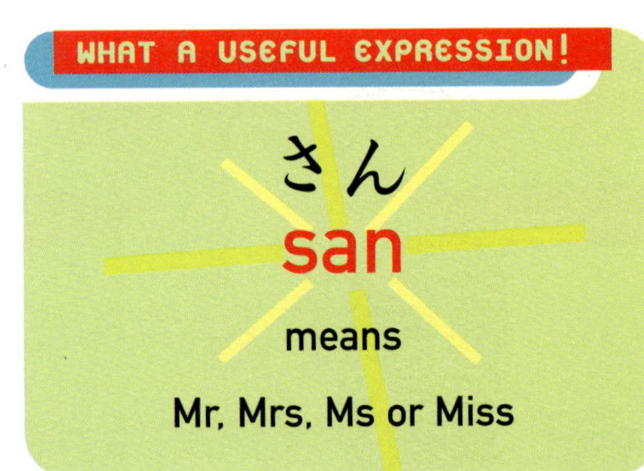

WHAT A USEFUL EXPRESSION!
さん
san
means
Mr, Mrs, Ms or Miss

Particles

ぼくは しんご です
Boku wa Shingo desu

That little word は **wa** in the sentence ぼくは しんご です **Boku wa Shingo desu** is called a particle. This は **wa** is the topic indicator. This means the word that is followed by は is the topic of the sentence. If the topic is obvious, you don't have to mention it. When introducing yourself, it is usually obvious that you are the topic, except when you are in a group.

You are the topic.
は
Me?

Introducing yourself

ひろ です。
Hiro desu.
どうぞ よろしく。
Dōzo yoroshiku.
シャロン です。
Sharon desu.
どうぞ よろしく。
Dōzo yoroshiku.

Introducing a school friend

ひろくん です。
Hiro-kun desu.
シャロンさん です。
Sharon-san desu.

Introducing adults

すずきさん です。
Suzuki-san desu.
スミスせんせい です。
Sumisu-sensei desu.
やまもとさん です。
Yamamoto-san desu.

Introducing yourself in a group

おなまえは？
Onamae wa?
ぼくは ベン です。
Boku wa Ben desu.
どうぞ よろしく。
Dōzo yoroshiku.
わたしは マリー です。
Watashi wa Marii desu.
どうぞ よろしく。
Dōzo yoroshiku.
わたしは キム です。
Watashi wa Kimu desu.
どうぞ よろしく。
Dōzo yoroshiku.

AB p. 4

できますか Dekimasuka CAN YOU DO IT?

1 Write down the names of these people as you hear them.

a  b  c  d 

2 Take turns. Pretend to be a well-known identity. Introduce yourself. Here are some suggestions.

* Batman
* Kathy Freeman
* Madonna
* Astro Boy

3 Form groups of five. Choose one person to be the tour guide (with any name you like). The guide is meeting Mr Tanaka and the members of the judo team at the airport.

* The guide introduces him/herself to the group.
* The group all introduce themselves to the guide.
* The guide introduces each person in the group to the rest of the class.

AIRPORT ARRIVALS
KIEKO
YAMADA
TANAKA
AKIRA

Note about names

Japanese names are usually said with the family name first, followed by the given name. For example, if Mr Aoi's given name is Hiro he might say *Aoi Hiro desu* or just *Aoi desu*. Children and teenagers usually introduce themselves to other young people by saying *either* their family name *or* their given name, but give their full name to adults.

Non-Japanese should say their name in their own way because Japanese people expect them to.

わかった！ Wakatta! I'VE GOT IT!

	Name	title	です	desu
Giving your name	Karen	—	です。	I'm Karen.
	Ken	—	です。	I'm Ken.
Introducing others	Karen	さん (san)	です。	This is Karen.
	Ken	くん (kun)	です。	This is Ken.
	Tanaka	せんせい (sensei)	です。	This is Mr/Mrs/Ms Tanaka.
	Jones	さん (san)	です。	This is Mr/Mrs/Ms Jones.
Giving your name in a group		ぼくは (Boku wa) Ken です。		(As for me) I'm Ken.
		わたしは (Watashi wa) Karen です。		(As for me) I'm Karen.
Meeting people		どうぞ よろしく。(Dōzo yoroshiku.)		Pleased to meet you.
		Ken です。どうぞ よろしく。		I'm Ken. Pleased to meet you.

べんきょう の こつ What's your secret?

Benkyō no kotsu

Karen, you can speak Japanese very well. How do you remember all the words? I learned the words for *Pleased to meet you* last week and now I can't remember them.

Well, everyone has different ways of remembering things. I have a visual memory, so I try to think of an English word or phrase that sounds a bit like the words I want to remember. I choose a word that I can put into a crazy scene in my mind. I then relate it to the word I want to remember. For example, you want to remember *Dōzo yoroshiku*, don't you? Well, I might think of bulldozer, a dozer because it sounds like *dōzo*. It has a brand name, SHIKU, on its side. I imagine it's saying, *Hi I'm a dozer*. I say, *Dozer you're a Shiku! Pleased to meet you!*

SHIKU
DOZER YOU'RE A SHIKU!

なに？　なに？

Nani? Nani?

What are they saying?

Shin
ぼくは　しん　です。
どうぞ　よろしく。
Chie
わたしは　ちえ　です。
どうぞ　よろしく。

Masahiko
まさひこ　です。
どうぞ
よろしく。
Yukari
ゆかり　です。
どうぞ
よろしく。

インフォ
Info
DID YOU KNOW?

Bowing

In Japan, people bow to each other in lots of circumstances. You will even see people bowing when talking on the phone!

When meeting for the first time ...

どうぞ　よろしく。
Dōzo yoroshiku.
たなか　です。よろしく。
Tanaka desu. Yoroshiku.

When greeting someone ...

こんにちは。
Konnichi wa.
せんせい、こんにちは。
Sensei, konnichi wa.

When saying goodbye ...

さようなら。
Sayōnara.

When offering food or a gift ...

どうぞ。
Dōzo.
ありがとう　ございます。
Arigatō gozaimasu.

... and thanking someone.

When apologising ...

すみません。
Sumimasen.

How *not* to bow!
Do it like this.

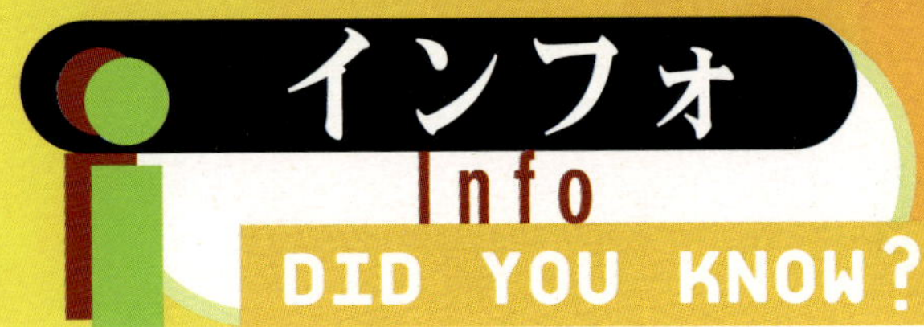
インフォ
Info
DID YOU KNOW?

Body language

Have you noticed that people often communicate with each other without using language? For example, think about the meaning of smiles, frowns and waving. This is called body language. Some body language has a universal meaning but, just as different communities around the world have developed different languages, so they have also developed different body languages. Japanese people are no exception. What do you do in the following circumstances?

Indicating yourself

Come this way, please.
Me?
Watashi?

Beckoning

Come here please! Kite kudasai.

Is she saying Goodbye?

Having your photo taken

Chiizu!
Cheese!

Saying no

Iie, iie.
No, no.

Listening attentively

Omoshiroi ...
Hm ... Interesting.

Meeting a friend after a long absence

Hisashiburi desu ne.
It's been such a long time!

QUIZ

What gestures do the following people use when they greet each other?

1 French people
2 Thai people
3 Japanese people
4 Maori people

Do you know any more?

あいさつ

Aisatsu

Greetings (I)

おはよう　ございます。
Ohayō gozaimasu.
おはよう。
Ohayō.

こんばんは。
Konban wa.

こんにちは。
Konnichi wa.

おやすみ　なさい。
Oyasumi nasai.

さようなら！
Sayōnara!

せつめい コーナー
Setsumei koonaa

Explanation corner

How do I say hello?

We say おはよう **Ohayō** or おはよう ございます **Ohayō gozaimasu** up to about 11 a.m. *Ohayō gozaimasu* originally meant *It is very early*.

Ohayō is informal, so we only say it to friends. It is a bit like the difference between *Hi!* and *Good morning*.

After 11 a.m. we usually say, こんにちは **Konnichi wa**. In the evening we say, こんばんは **Konban wa**.

How do I say goodbye?

When saying goodbye we sometimes say さようなら **Sayōnara**, but if we see the person often we usually say, じゃ、また **Ja, mata** or また あした **Mata ashita**. This is a bit like *See you soon* or *See you tomorrow*.

We say おやすみ なさい **Oyasumi nasai** at bedtime. It is a bit like *Sleep well*.

できますか

Dekimasuka
CAN YOU DO IT?

1 Kitsune points to one of the characters and one of the clocks.
Tanuki greets the person indicated.
Kitsune returns the greeting.

21:00

8:45

15:00

13:00

7:30

23:50

Keiko, a friend

Mr Akimoto, a neighbour

Mrs Yamada, a neighbour

Akira, a friend

Miss Nakamura, a teacher

2 Listen to the conversations. Circle true (T) or false (F) according to what you hear.

a	They are meeting in the early morning.	T	F
b	They are meeting in the evening.	T	F
c	One of them is going to bed.	T	F
d	A student is greeting a teacher.	T	F
e	Friends are saying goodbye.	T	F
f	They are meeting in the afternoon.	T	F
g	Friends are meeting in the early morning.	T	F
h	They are saying goodbye.	T	F

3 Choose from the following greetings, and place the appropriate number of the greeting in the relevant speech bubble. You will need to put more than one number in some bubbles.

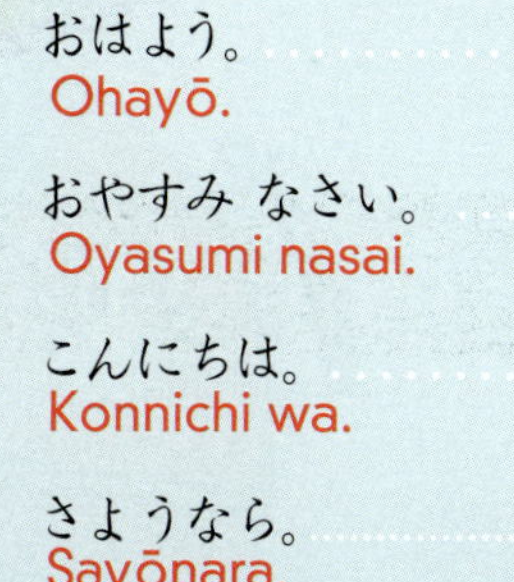

おはよう。 (1)
Ohayō.

おやすみ なさい。 (2)
Oyasumi nasai.

こんにちは。 (3)
Konnichi wa.

さようなら。 (4)
Sayōnara.

こんばんは。 (5)
Konban wa.

じゃ、また。 (6)
Ja, mata.

おはよう ございます。 (7)
Ohayō gozaimasu.

ゲーム Game

Play *janken* with your partner to decide who wins.

Rules

Stone defeats scissors; scissors defeats paper; paper defeats stone.

If you win with a stone advance one place; with scissors two places; with paper three.

Use two different coins as the markers.

- If you land on a square with a picture of a bird you must say, おはよう ございます Ohayō gozaimasu.
- If you land on a square with a picture of the sun you must say, こんにちは Konnichi wa.
- If you land on a square with a picture of the moon you must say, こんばんは Konban wa.
- If you land on a square with a picture of a hand you must say, さようなら Sayōnara.
- If you land on a square with a picture of a bed you must say, おやすみ なさい Oyasumi nasai.

Start!

Coin 5¢

Coin 5¢

Finish!

If you say the wrong greeting or cannot remember the right one, you miss a turn. The winner is the one who finishes first.

わかった！ Wakatta! I'VE GOT IT!

	Name	Title	Informal	Polite
Morning greeting	—	-さん -san -くん -kun -せんせい -sensei	おはよう Ohayō	おはよう ございます Ohayō gozaimasu
Saying goodbye			じゃ、また Ja, mata また あした Mata ashita	さようなら Sayōnara
Afternoon greeting				こんにちは Konnichi wa
Evening greeting				こんばんは Konban wa
Goodnight				おやすみ なさい Oyasumi nasai

うたいましょう Let's sing!

Utaimashō

Sing your name in the gap.

おはよう みなさん [Your Name] で — す
Ohayō minasan ______de — su
こんにちは みなさん [Your Name] で — す
Konnichi wa minasan ______de — su
どうぞ よろしく— こ
Dōzo yoroshi — ku
1
2
Chorus
(Good evening)
こんばんは (Good night)
Konban wa
Chorus
お — やすみなさい
O — yasumi nasai
さようなら せんせ — い
Sayōnara sense — i
さようなら
Sayōnara
さような— ら
Sayōna— ra

ひらがな Hiragana

わ	た	し	は
wa	ta (だ da)	shi (じ ji)	ha (wa)
わ for wire	た for tap	し for shield	は for hanky

て	す	ほ	く
te (で de)	su (ず zu)	ho (ぼ bo)	ku (ぐ gu)
て for tent	す for snail	ほ for a hole in a tree	く for Pac-Man

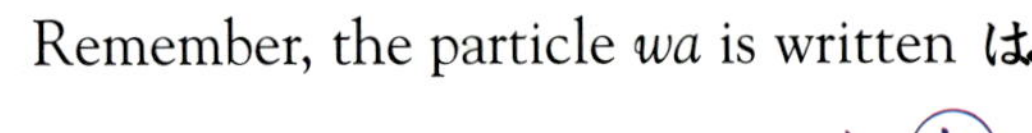
Remember, the particle *wa* is written は.

あ	か	さ	(た)	な	(は)	ま	や	ら	(わ)	ん
い	き	(し)	ち	に	ひ	み		り		
う	(く)	(す)	つ	ぬ	ふ	む	ゆ	る		
え	け	せ	(て)	ね	へ	め		れ		
お	こ	そ	と	の	(ほ)	も	よ	ろ	を	

AB pp. 6–8

ひらがな れんしゅう
Hiragana renshuu

Hiragana exercises

1 Write the correct hiragana in the boxes.

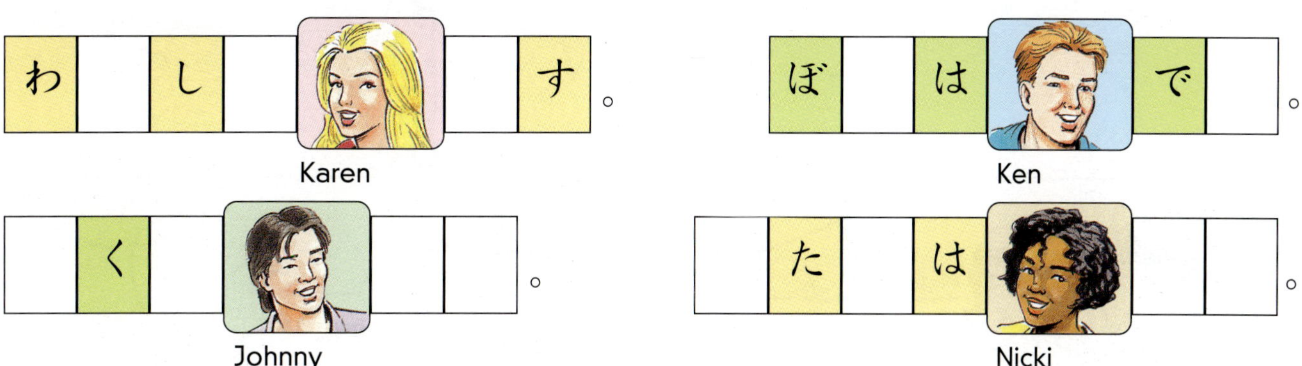
わ
し
す
。
Karen
ぼ
は
で
。
Ken
く
。
Johnny
た
は
。
Nicki

2 Choose the correct word from the boxes and circle it.

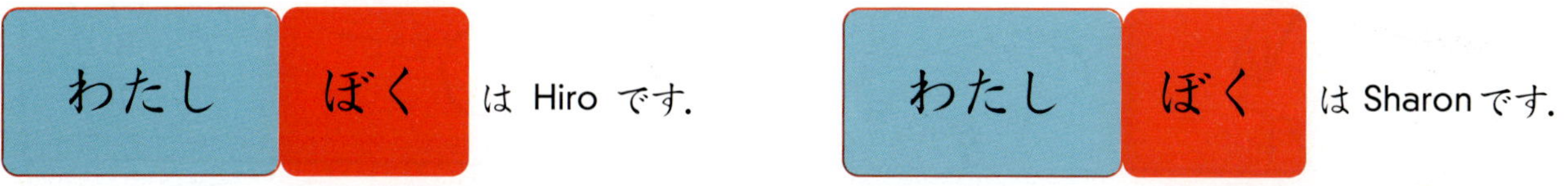
わたし
ぼく
は Hiro です.
わたし
ぼく
は Sharon です.

3 Look at the rainbow over Hiragana Mountain!

How many わ can you find? How many た can you find? How many し can you find? How many は can you find?
How many で can you find? How many す can you find? How many ぼ can you find?
And how many く can you find?
わたしは
あした、やまへ
いくんです。とても たの
しみです。ぼくは きのう、うみへ いって
すいかを たべたんです。すごく おいしかったです。

てんせい

★✣★✤☆...
(さようなら ...)

こんにちは。

こんにちは。

こんにちは。

たく です。
どうぞ よろしく。

しほ です。
どうぞ
よろしく。

てんせい です。
どうぞ
よろしく。

Woof! Woof!
です です。
どうぞ よろしく。

✤❣❋☆✾ ✸✳❞✌⊞!!!!
Mission completed!

AB p. 9

チェック しましょう!
Chekku shimashō!

Let's check!

Titles	
～くん kun	Mr/Master (males your own age)
～さん san	Mr/Mrs/Mrs
～せんせい sensei	Mr/Mrs/Ms (a teacher)

Pronouns	
ぼく	I (informal, a male speaking)
わたし	I (formal, male or female speaking)

Boku
Watashi

Expressions for introductions	
おなまえは? Onamae wa?	Your name is?
どうぞ よろしく Dōzo yoroshiku	Pleased to meet you
です	is, am, are

People	
せんせい sensei	teacher
みなさん minasan	everyone

Greetings	
おはよう Ohayō!	~~Hi!~~ Good morning
おはよう ございます Ohayō gozaimasu	Good morning
おやすみ なさい Oyasumi nasai	Good night
こんにちは Konnichi wa	Hello Good afternoon
こんばんは Konban wa	Good evening
さようなら Sayōnara	Goodbye
じゃ、また Ja, mata	See you
また あした Mata ashita	See you tomorrow

I can:

- ◯ say my name and introduce myself
- ◯ introduce my friends
- ◯ ask someone's name
- ◯ say good morning
- ◯ say hello or good afternoon
- ◯ say goodnight
- ◯ say goodbye to friends and strangers
- ◯ understand particle は
- ◯ read and write ぼくは ～ です。
わたしは ～ です。

Unit
2

なんさい ですか

Nan-sai desuka

How old are you?

1

1 2 3 4 5 6
ichi ni san shi go roku
7 8 9 10!
shichi hachi kyuu juu!

2

3

カレンさん。
Karen san.

はい。
Hai.

4

みょうじは　なん　ですか。
Myōji wa nan desuka.

スコット　です。
Sukotto desu.

5

でんわばんごうは　なん　ばん　ですか。
Denwa-bangō wa nan-ban desuka.

5468－1372 です。
Go yon roku hachi no ichi san nana ni desu.

6
なん　さい　ですか。
Nan-sai desuka.
17 さい　です。
Juunana-sai desu.
7
ジョニーくんも 17 さい　ですか。
Jonii-kun mo juunana-sai desuka.
はい、ぼくも 17 さい　です。
Hai, boku mo juunana-sai desu.
8
ひろくんも 17 さい　ですか。
Hiro-kun mo juunana-sai desuka.
いいえ、ぼくは 16 さい　です。
Iie, boku wa juuroku-sai desu.
9
じゃ、ジョニーくん、カレンさん。
Ja, Jonii-kun, Karen-san.
はい！
Hai!
10

できますか
Dekimasuka
CAN YOU DO IT?

Can you find …

* how to count to ten?
* how to ask for someone's phone number?
* how to ask how old someone is?
* the word for surname?

せつめい コーナー
Setsumei koonaa
Explanation corner

Counting

You will have to learn the words for counting to ten, but after that it is easy. For example:

eleven is **juuichi** (10 + 1)
twelve is **juuni** (10 + 2)
thirteen is **juusan** (10 + 3)
and so on until you get to twenty, which is **nijuu** (2 tens).

Twenty-one is **nijuuichi** (2 tens + 1)
thirty is **sanjuu** (3 tens)
forty is **yonjuu** (4 tens)
forty-three is **yonjuusan** (4 tens + 3) and
fifty is **gojuu** (5 tens).

Keep going like this until you get to one hundred, which is **hyaku**.

Saying your age

To say your age, just add さい **sai** to the number of years. さい means *years old*. We use よん **yon** and なな **nana** instead of し **shi** and しち **shichi,** for four and seven. This is because *shi* can also mean *death* and *shichi* can mean *into the jaws of death*. In the past, people thought these numbers were unlucky. Some people still think these numbers are unlucky. Are there any numbers in English that people think are unlucky?

By the way, look out for changes in the way you pronounce numbers when giving ages. Have a look at the chart opposite. Can you guess why there are these phonetic changes?

WHAT A USEFUL EXPRESSION!

か
ka

When you hear *ka* at the end of a sentence, you have just heard a question!

ka = ?

AB p. 10

かぞえましょう

Let's count!

Kazoemashō!

1 to 10			
1	一	ichi	
2	二	ni	
3	三	san	
4	四	shi	
5	五	go	
6	六	roku	
7	七	shichi	
8	八	hachi	
9	九	kyuu	
10	十	juu	

11 to 20		
11	十一	juuichi
12	十二	juuni
13	十三	juusan
14	十四	juushi
15	十五	juugo
16	十六	juuroku
17	十七	juushichi
18	十八	juuhachi
19	十九	juukyuu
20	二十	nijuu

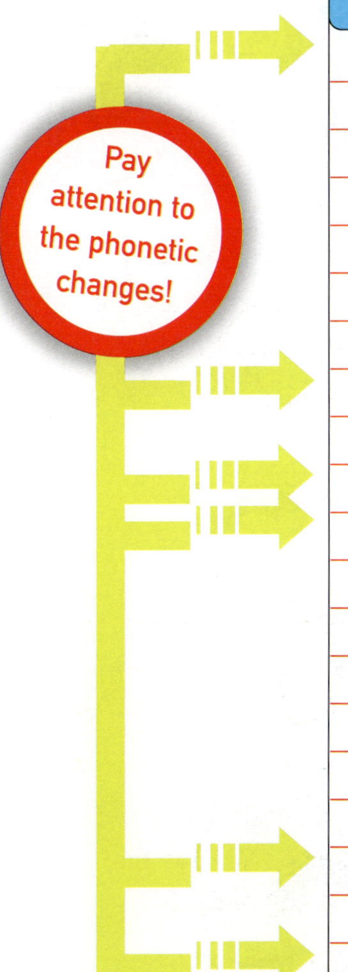
Pay attention to the phonetic changes!

Ages up to 20		
1さい	一さい	is-sai
2さい	二さい	ni-sai
3さい	三さい	san-sai
4さい	四さい	yon-sai
5さい	五さい	go-sai
6さい	六さい	roku-sai
7さい	七さい	nana-sai
8さい	八さい	has-sai
9さい	九さい	kyuu-sai
10さい	十さい	jus-sai
11さい	十一さい	juuis-sai
12さい	十二さい	juuni-sai
13さい	十三さい	juusan-sai
14さい	十四さい	juuyon-sai
15さい	十五さい	juugo-sai
16さい	十六さい	juuroku-sai
17さい	十七さい	juunana-sai
18さい	十八さい	juuhas-sai
19さい	十九さい	juukyuu-sai
20さい	二十さい／はたち	nijus-sai/hatachi

Do not say *shi-sai*.

Never say *ku-sai*. Never! (Ask your teacher for the secret reason.)

Special name for 20 years old.

Particles

ぼくも 17さい です
Boku mo 17-sai desu

That little word も *mo* in the sentence ジョニーくんも 17さい です **Jonii-kun mo 17-sai desu** is another particle. The sentence means either *Johnny too is 17* or *Johnny is 17 too*. In Japanese the particle always follows the word it belongs to, as it does in the first English sentence, *Johnny too is 17*.

You too!
も
Me too!

Asking and giving ages

なん さい ですか。
Nan-sai desuka.
14 さい です。
Juuyon-sai desu.

Saying your age is the same

なん さい ですか。
Nan-sai desuka.
ぼくも 14 さい です。
Boku mo juuyon-sai desu.

Giving your age in a group

なん さい ですか。
Nan-sai desuka.
13 さい です。
Juusan-sai desu.
わたしも 13 さい です。
Watashi mo juusan-sai desu.
ぼくは 14 さい です。
Boku wa juuyon-sai desu.
わたしは 12 さい です。
Watashi wa juuni-sai desu.
ぼくも 12 さい です。
Boku mo juuni-sai desu.

AB p. 10

できますか
Dekimasuka
CAN YOU DO IT?

1 Select the panel

These people have applied to be panelists in a quiz show. The show has three divisions:

- ✱ Division A: under 12 years old
- ✱ Division B: 13–18 years old
- ✱ Division C: 19 years old and over

Listen for their names and ages and fill out the table.

Name	Age	Division
Sasaki		
Ueda		
Murayama		
Ikeda		
Morita		
Sakashita		
Nakamura		

2 ESP—Can you tune in?

Take turns with a partner.

- ✱ Choose one of the ages shown in the ring.
- ✱ Concentrate on the age and try to send it in Japanese to your partner by thought transference.
- ✱ Your partner should try to tune in to your thoughts and attempt to choose the same age for themselves.

Juugo-sai desu.

Boku wa juuyon-sai desu.

15 30 19 21
33 16 25 24
18 20 14 17

Watashi wa juugo-sai desu.

3 Amida kuji

Amida kuji is a special game which is played in Japan to make fair and random decisions. For example, to decide who will be partners in a game, parallel lines are drawn down a page and random cross lines added. The names of half of the players are written on the bottom of the page and covered up. The rest of the students choose an end and follow it down and across every line until they find their partner.

Ken Don May Len Ros Pat

Use the *Amida kuji* method to find out how old these people are. Tell your partner in Japanese.
For example: Shingo-san wa _____ -sai desu.

Morita
Shingo
Kaoru
Tatsuya
Seiko
Michiko
20
37
43
18
13
14

わかった Wakatta! I'VE GOT IT!

Counting	Use し shi for four and しち shichi for seven.			
Saying your age	Add さい sai to your age. Use よん yon and なな nana for four and seven.			
Agreeing	はい、 Hai,	わたしも or ぼくも watashi mo or boku mo	same information	です。 desu.
Disagreeing	いいえ、 Iie,	わたしは or ぼくは watashi wa or boku wa	different information	です。 desu.

あそびましょう！ Just for fun!

Asobimashō!

てるてるぼうず Teru teru bōzu is a charm which children make to encourage fine weather. During *Tsuyu* (rainy season), everyone gets tired of the endless rainy days. Sometimes a fine day is needed for excursions or sports. At such times, people make a てるてるぼうず teru teru bōzu and hang it near a window.

Try your hand at making one.

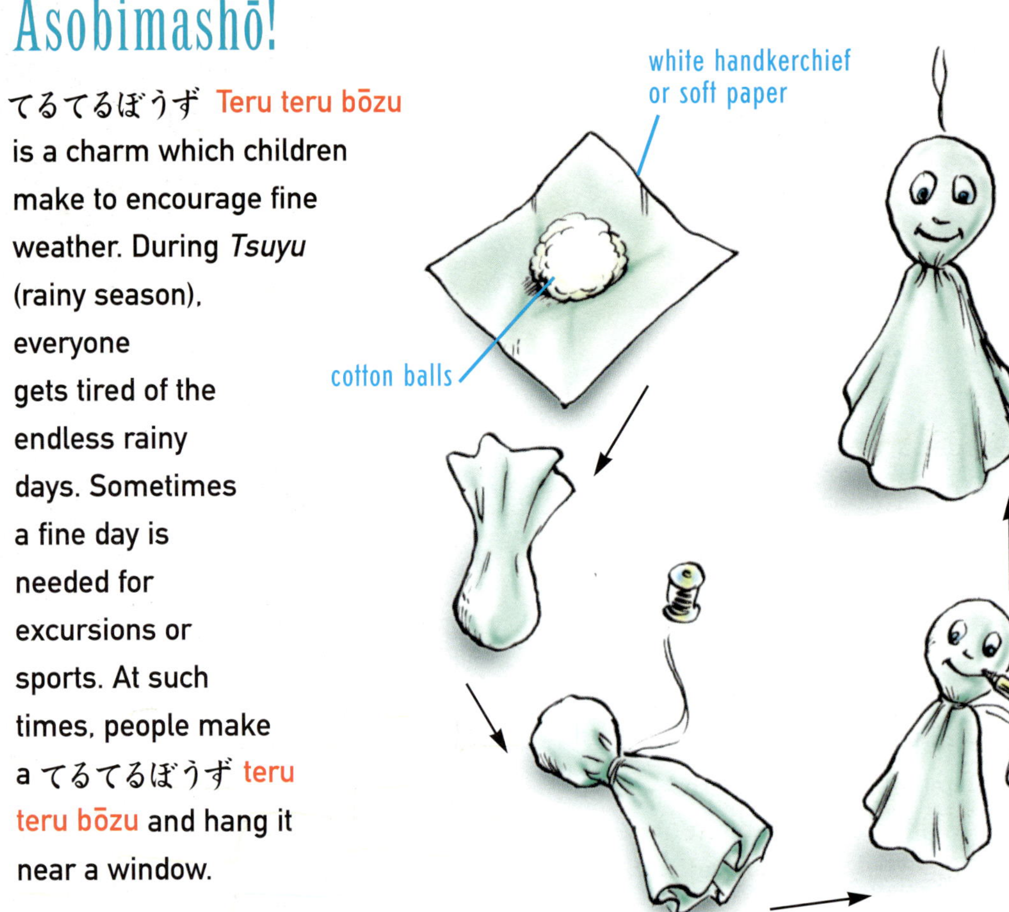

white handkerchief or soft paper
cotton balls

なに？ なに？

Nani? Nani?

What are they saying?

7さい です。
5さい です。

8さい です。

12さい です。
なんさい ですか。

15さい です。

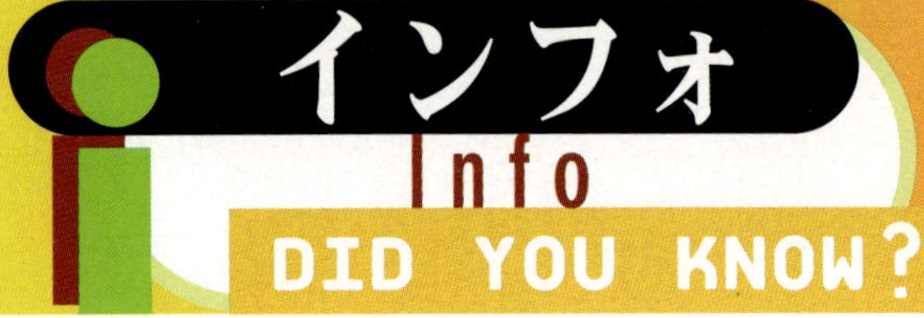
インフォ
Info
DID YOU KNOW?

Family names

What Japanese names do you know?

Sushi
Toyota
Inoue
Teriyaki
Tanaka
Suzuki
Mitsubishi
Ikeda

Are these all correct? Which names are not family names?

- Japanese family names are usually written in kanji and have meanings. The meanings often relate to where the family lived long ago, just like many English family names.
- Many Japanese people use a business card, called a *meishi*, when they introduce themselves. It is particularly important for business people, because the card usually states which company they work for.
- Japanese people use a stamp, called an *inkan*, when they are required to give a signature. This stamp is specially made with the family name in kanji carved on it.

Name	Kanji	Meaning
Mori	森	forest
Yamada	山田	mountain paddy
Takahashi	高橋	high bridge
Kitagawa	北川	north river
Nishimura	西村	west village
Ishihara	石原	stony field
Kobayashi	小林	little wood

学校法人
メリノール女子学院
メリノール女子学院中・高等学校教諭
コネル・スペンサー・ジョン
四日市市平尾町二八〇〇
電話〈〇五九三〉二六―〇〇六七番

A *meishi*

山田

An *inkan*

AB pp. 14, 17

Kanji numbers

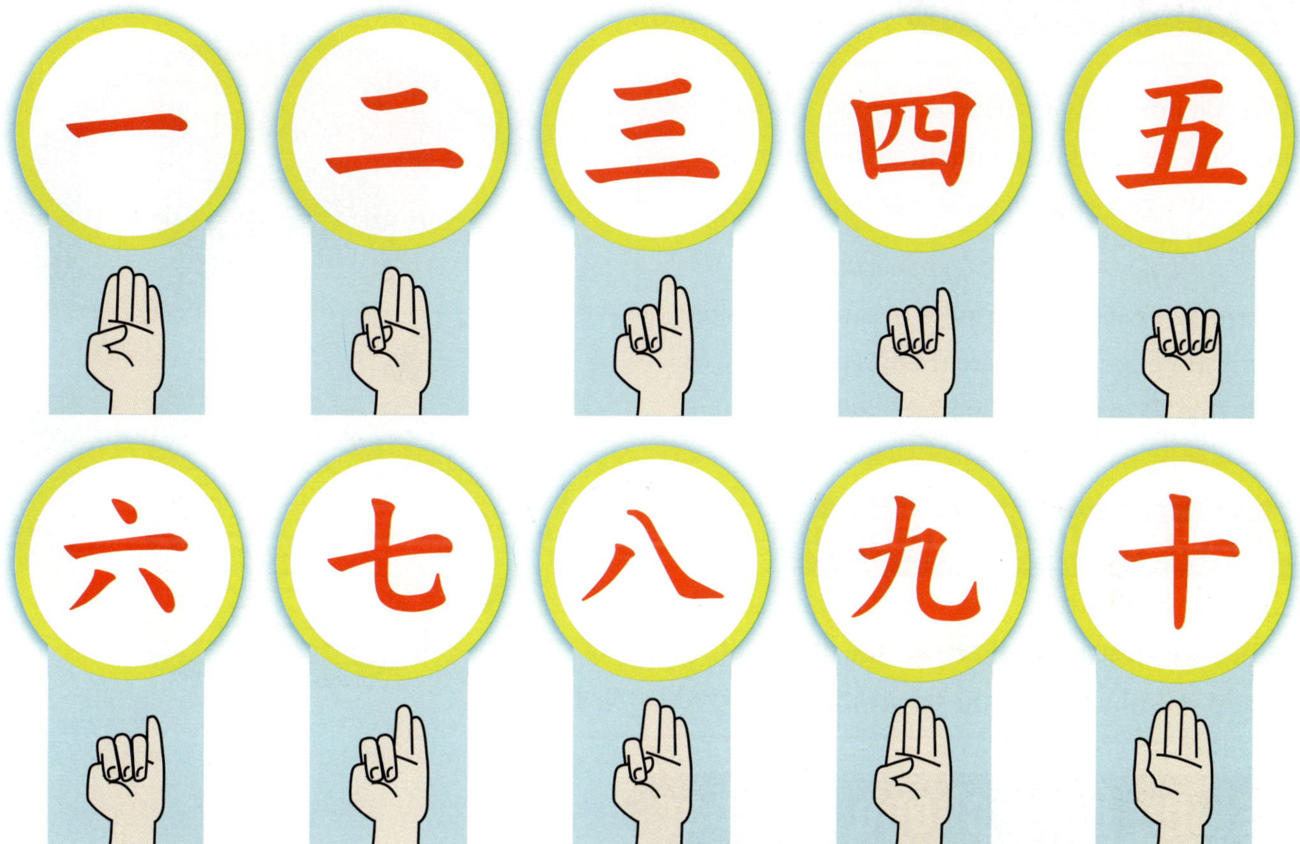
一
二
三
四
五
六
七
八
九
十

Numbers can be written using the kanji shown above. You can learn them for fun. However, nowadays Roman numbers are more widely used. Can you guess when kanji numbers are used?

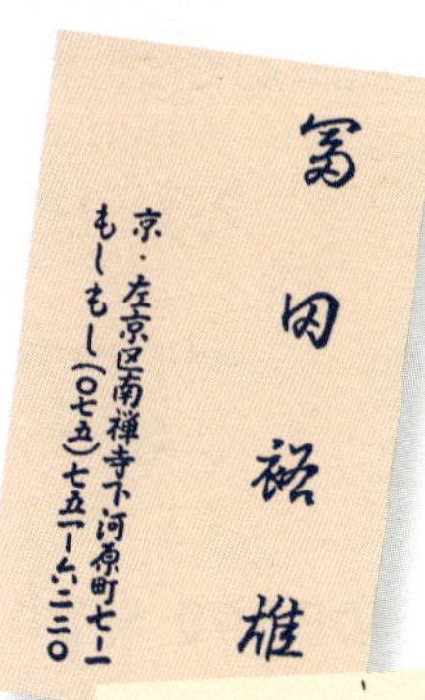
京・左京区南禅寺下河原町七一
もしもし(〇七五)七五一—六二二〇

5　つぎの数を，下の数直線に↓であらわしなさい。
また，↑のところの数を小数で書きなさい。

0.2　$\frac{3}{10}$　$\frac{8}{10}$　1.6　2.1

0　1　2

①　②　③　④　⑤

6　つぎの計算をしなさい。

① $7095 + 6928$　$24567 + 5439$　$8204 - 3427$　$47000 - 17908$

② 215×9　627×47　870×32　508×50

③ $5\overline{)95}$　$3\overline{)62}$　$6\overline{)882}$　$7\overline{)576}$

$8\overline{)832}$　$2\overline{)753}$　$9\overline{)9059}$　$5\overline{)3502}$

④ $\frac{1}{5}+\frac{3}{5}$　$\frac{4}{8}+\frac{1}{8}$　$\frac{7}{9}-\frac{2}{9}$　$1-\frac{2}{7}$

⑤ $0.5+0.6$　$1.4+0.8$　$2.7+1.5$

$0.8-0.3$　$2-0.6$　$3.1-1.4$

83

品川53
ふ96-18

せつめい コーナー
Setsumei koonaa

Explanation corner

Phone numbers

Did you notice that when we give our phone numbers we just say the numbers one after the other. We also say *zero* for 0, just like you do.

We use よん **yon** and なな **nana** for four and seven. You need to remember to say の **no** after the district codes or where there is a dash. By the way, this の **no** is pronounced like the *no* in *not*.

Answering the phone

When we answer the phone we usually say もしもし **Moshi moshi** and then the family name followed by です.

Asking for a phone number

When we ask for someone's phone number we say でんわ ばんごうは なん ばん ですか. **Denwa-bangō wa nan-ban desuka.**

The word for phone is でんわ **denwa** and for number is ばんごう **bangō**. なん ばん **Nan-ban** means *What number?* The *ban* is short for *bangō*.

Asking for someone's phone number

Giving your phone number

でんわ ばんごうは なん ばん ですか。
Denwa-bangō wa nan-ban desuka.
674-380 です。
Roku nana yon no san hachi zero desu.
でんわ ばんごうは 673-042 です。
Denwa-bangō wa roku nana san no zero yon ni desu.

AB p. 11

できますか Dekimasuka CAN YOU DO IT?

1 This salesperson is writing down customers' phone numbers. If she repeats correctly give her a tick, if not give her a cross.

1 ☐ 2 ☐ 3 ☐
4 ☐ 5 ☐ 6 ☐

2 Write down the telephone numbers of the following take-away food shops.

☎ ________ Chicken Dinner	☎ ________ Super Noodles
☎ ________ Macburgers	☎ ________ Pizza Delight
☎ ________ Curry House	☎ ________ Fish 'n' Chips

3 Mixed identity

Take turns with a partner.

Kitsune starts.

- Choose a name from list A.
- Choose an age from list B.
- Choose a telephone number from list C. Write down your choices secretly.

Tanuki must find out the information by asking questions and then fill in the form. *Example:*

Tanuki: Onamae wa?
Kitsune: Uchiyama desu.
Tanuki: Nan-sai desuka.
Kitsune: Juuni-sai desu.
Tanuki: Denwa-bangō wa nan-ban desuka.
Kitsune: Hachi ni ichi no san yon hachi desu.

A	Yamashita	Uchiyama	Katō	Nakamura	Hirata
B	17	20	12	14	18
C	678-984	783-921	821-348	376-104	209-673

なまえ Namae	ねんれい Nenrei (age)	でんわ ばんごう Denwa-bangō
________	________	________

かずのゲーム

Kazu no geemu

Number game

Play *janken* with your partner instead of throwing dice. If you win with a stone advance one place; with scissors two places; and with paper five places. Use two different coins as the markers.

- If you land on a square with a picture of annual growth rings of a tree with a question mark, you must say なん　さい　ですか。Nan-sai desuka.
- If you land on a square with a picture of annual growth rings of a tree, you must say your age in Japanese.
- If you land on a square with a picture of a telephone with a question mark, you must say でんわ　ばんごうは　なん　ばん　ですか。Denwa-bangō wa nan-ban desuka.
- If you land on a square with a picture of a telephone, you must say your telephone number in Japanese.
- If you land on a square with a numeral, you must say that number in Japanese.

Start!
5
2
6
9
3
1
4
7
12
10
8
13
Finish!

わかった！ Wakatta! I'VE GOT IT!

Asking for someone's phone number	でんわ　ばんごうは　なん　ばん　ですか。 Denwa-bangō wa nan-ban desuka.
Giving your phone number	✧ Say the numbers as separate numbers. ✧ Say *zero* for 0. ✧ Use よん yon and なな nana for four and seven. ✧ Put の no after the district codes or where there is a dash.

なに？　なに？ Nani? Nani?

What are they saying?

でんわ　ばんごうは　なん　ばん　ですか。
でんわ　ばんごうは 1247-3260 です。
でんわ　ばんごうは　なん　ばん　ですか。
ええと、346-2851 です。

ひらがな

Hiragana

さ	ざ	い	ん	ぱ	は	ば
sa	za	i	n	pa	ha	ba

さ for sandal

い for eagle

ん is for saying 'nnn …'

は for hanky

こ	ご	う	も
ko	go	u	mo

こ for cockatoo

う for oozing

も for mop

Remember: the vowel *o* is almost always extended using う, as in でんわ ばんごう **denwa-bangō.**

ん	わ	ら	や	ま	は	な	た	さ	か	あ
		り		み	ひ	に	ち	し	き	い
		る	ゆ	む	ふ	ぬ	つ	す	く	う
		れ		め	へ	ね	て	せ	け	え
	を	ろ	よ	も	ほ	の	と	そ	こ	お

ひらがな れんしゅう
Hiragana renshuu

Hiragana exercises

1 Write the correct hiragana in the squares.

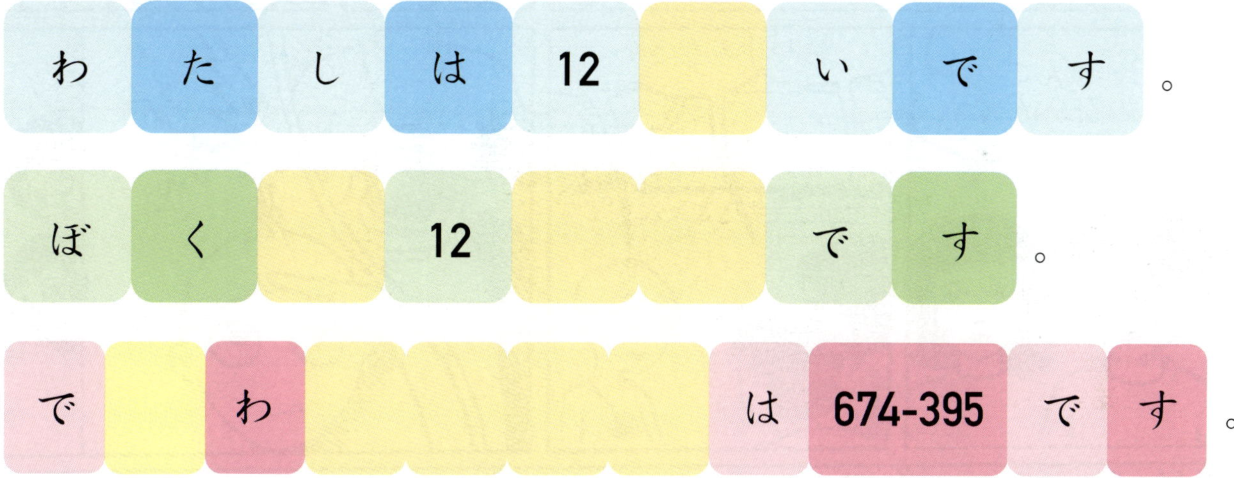
わ た し は 12 い で す 。
ぼ く 12 で す 。
で わ は 674-395 で す 。

2 Join the hiragana with the correct roomaji.

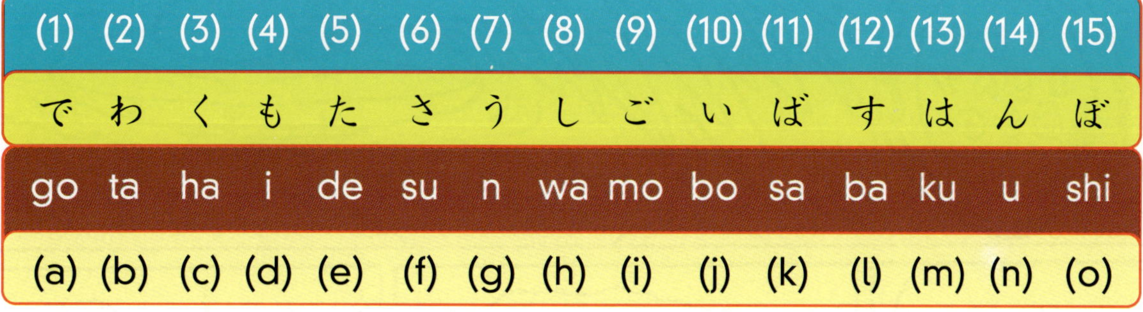

(1)	(2)	(3)	(4)	(5)	(6)	(7)	(8)	(9)	(10)	(11)	(12)	(13)	(14)	(15)
で	わ	く	も	た	さ	う	し	ご	い	ば	す	は	ん	ぼ
go	ta	ha	i	de	su	n	wa	mo	bo	sa	ba	ku	u	shi
(a)	(b)	(c)	(d)	(e)	(f)	(g)	(h)	(i)	(j)	(k)	(l)	(m)	(n)	(o)

3 Say as many of the hiragana in the river as possible aloud to your partner. Circle all the fish you can 'catch'.

さ
ば
ん
ぼ
ご
い
ご
う
ん
も
ご
ぼ
も
ば
い
う
ば

てんせい

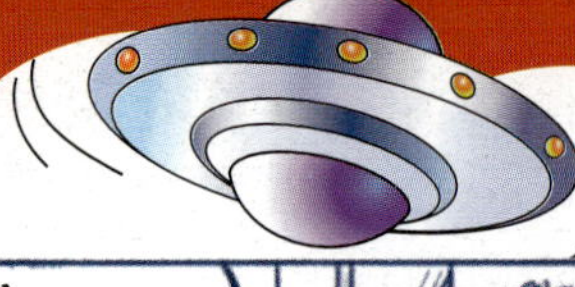

なん さい
ですか。

12 さい
です。

でんわ ばんごうは
なん ばん ですか。

でんわ ばんごうは
722 の 35946 です。

おやすみなさい

1 2 3
4 5 6 7
8 9 0
Receiving! Receiving!

(でんわ ばんご うは
722 の 35946...)

GOOD LUCK!

AB p. 18

チェック しましょう!
Chekku shimashō!

Let's check!

Suffixes	
〜さい	~years old
〜ばん	~number

Expressions	
もしもし Moshi moshi	Hello (on the phone)

Question words	
なん nan	what
なん さい	what age
なん ばん	what number
か	?

Answer words	
いいえ iie	no
はい	yes

Personal information	
でんわ ばんごう	telephone number
みょうじ myōji	surname

I can:

- ◯ count to 20 or more
- ◯ say my age
- ◯ ask others' ages and understand the reply
- ◯ say my phone number
- ◯ understand phone numbers
- ◯ say yes and no
- ◯ recognise five Japanese family names
- ◯ read and write なん さい ですか ...
- ◯ ... and でんわ ばんごうは なん ばん ですか。

9
8
7
6
5
4
3
2
1

Unit 3

どこに すんで いますか

Doko ni sunde imasuka

Where do you live?

1 At the end of the lesson …

everyone bows to the teacher.

2

せんせい、さようなら。
Sensei, sayōnara.

さようなら。
Sayōnara.

3

TANAKA JUDO ACADEMY

カレン さん！
Karen-san!

4

なん さい ですか。
Nan-sai desuka.

17 さい です。
Juunana-sai desu.

ぼくも。
Boku mo.

5

どこに すんで いますか。
Doko ni sunde imasuka.

ROBINA

ゴードンに すんで います。
Gōdon ni sunde imasu.

6
To Robina
To Gordon
We are here
ぼくは ロビナに
Boku wa Robina ni
すんで います。
sunde imasu.
7
じゃ、また。
Ja, mata.
8
カレン さん、アメリカじん ですか。
Karen-san, Amerika-jin desuka.
いいえ、カナダじん です。
Iie, Kanada-jin desu.
ああ、そう ですか。
Aa, sō desuka.
9
どこに すんで いますか。
Doko ni sunde imasuka.
ゴードンに すんで います。
Gōdon ni sunde imasu.
BUS STOP
73 GORDON
10
ぼくも ゴードンに すんで います。
Boku mo Gōdon ni sunde imasu!

できますか
Dekimasuka
CAN YOU DO IT?

Can you find …

* Where Karen lives?
* Where Ken lives?
* What nationality Karen is?
* How old Ken is?
* Where Johnny lives?

せつめい コーナー
Setsumei koonaa

Explanation corner

How do I say where I live?

To ask where someone lives say, どこに すんで いますか。 **Doko ni sunde imasuka.** When I asked Yukari where she lived I said, ゆかりさん、どこに すんで いますか。 **Yukari-san, doko ni sunde imasuka.** She answered, きょうとに すんで います。 **Kyōto ni sunde imasu** because she lives in Kyōto.

To answer, you just replace the question word どこ **doko** with the answer and keep the rest of the sentence the same. Of course, you leave off the question mark か **ka**!

How do I say my nationality?

To say your nationality, put じん **jin,** which means person, after the name of your country. For example, アメリカじん です。 **Amerika-jin desu.** *I'm an American.*

To ask if someone comes from a particular country add じん **jin** to the name of the country and then make a question with ですか **desuka**. For example, アメリカじん ですか。 **Amerika-jin desuka.** *Are you an American?*

America and Canada fit the Japanese syllabary very neatly but other countries have to be changed quite a bit. Can you guess what these countries are?

- Doitsu
- Oosutoraria
- Nyuujiirando
- Igirisu
- Girisha
- Oranda
- Mareeshia

By the way, if you want to know someone's country of birth, say, おくには どこ ですか。 **Okuni wa doko desuka.**

WHAT A USEFUL EXPRESSION!

ああ そう ですか。
Aa, sō desuka.

To keep the conversation going, just keep saying it!

It means *Really? Is that right?*

Particles

おおさかに すんで います
Oosaka ni sunde imasu

The particle に **ni** can have several meanings. You will learn about the other meanings later. In the sentence **ゴードンに すんで います Gōdon ni sunde imasu,** the particle に indicates the place where someone lives. It is similar to *in* or *at* in English.

Place
に
ni
to be (in)
to live (in)

Asking where someone lives

どこに すんで いますか。
Doko ni sunde imasuka.
シドニーに すんで います。
Shidonii ni sunde imasu.

Guessing nationality

インドネシアじん ですか。
Indoneshia-jin desuka.
日本語
いいえ、マレーシアじん です。
Iie, Mareeshia-jin desu.

Asking for someone's country of birth

おくには どこ ですか。
Okuni wa doko desuka.
オーストラリア です。
Oosutoraria desu.

Saying your nationality

オーストラリアじん です。
Oosutoraria-jin desu.
にほんじん です。
Nihon-jin desu.
フランスじん です。
Furansu-jin desu.

AB p. 19

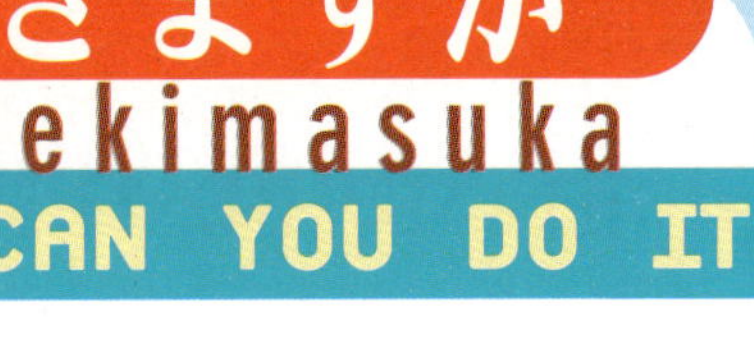
できますか

Dekimasuka

CAN YOU DO IT?

1 Fill in the survey form about the contestants in the quiz show.

Name	Age	Nationality

2 Using the *Amida kuji* game, take turns to say the nationality of the following people.

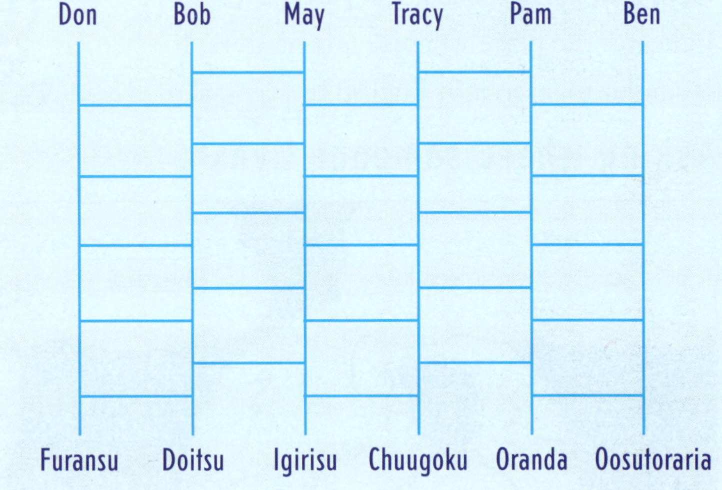

Don
Bob
May
Tracy
Pam
Ben
Furansu
Doitsu
Igirisu
Chuugoku
Oranda
Oosutoraria

3 Take turns with a partner.

Kitsune is the game show host and asks the questions. Tanuki is the contestant and must choose answers from the list. Kitsune then tells the class all about Tanuki.

Game show host

Find out the following:

- where the contestant lives
- name
- age
- country of birth
- phone number.

Contestant

Choose from the following:

Akira

Seiko

Suzuko

Hiro

Naomi

Saburo

16
14
18
20
32
13

Nihon
Chuugoku
Itaria
Oosutoraria
Igirisu
Nyuujiirando

Tōkyō
Kyōto
Oosaka
Sapporo
Nagoya
Takayama

Make up a phone number.

4 Take turns to say where each train traveller lives.

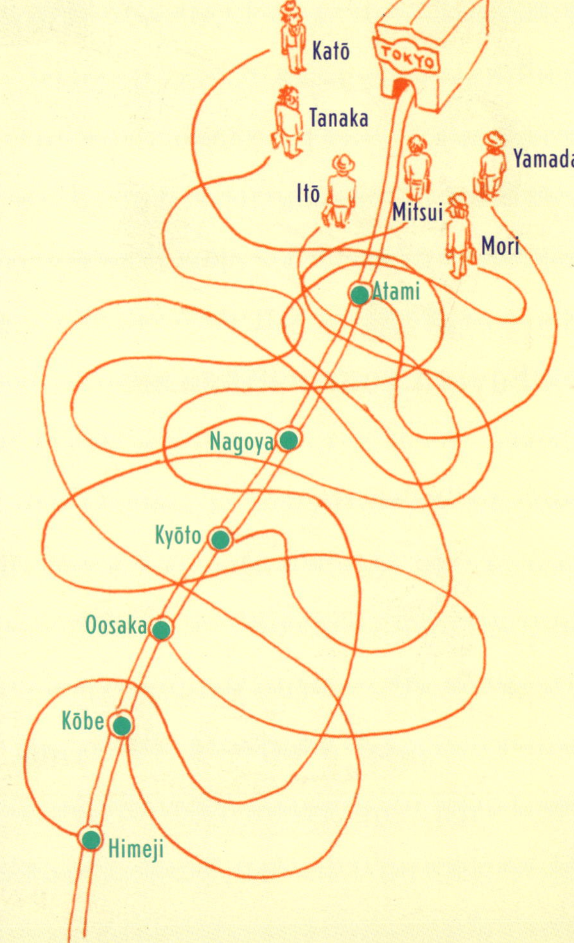

Tōkyō
TOKYO
Katō
Tanaka
Yamada
Itō
Mitsui
Mori
Atami
Nagoya
Kyōto
Oosaka
Kōbe
Himeji

おくには どこ ですか
Okuni wa doko desuka

Where are you from?

Play *janken* with your partner.

If you win with a stone, advance one place; with scissors two places; with paper three places.

Use two coins as the counters.

Whichever flag you land on, your partner must say, おくには どこ ですか。Okuni wa doko desuka.

You should answer the question, then say your assumed nationality and where you live.

For example, you land on Italy, so you say:

イタリア です。イタリアじん です。イタリアに すんで います。
Itaria desu. Itaria-jin desu. Itaria ni sunde imasu.

If you make a mistake, move back two places. The winner is the one who reaches the end first.

Start

1 イギリス Igirisu
2 フランス Furansu
3 にほん Nihon
4 ギリシャ Girisha
5 オランダ Oranda
6 マレーシア Mareeshia
7  オーストラリア Oosutoraria
8  ちゅうごく Chuugoku
9  カナダ Kanada
10  インドネシア Indoneshia
11  イタリア Itaria
12  ニュージーランド Nyuujiirando

みなさん、どこに すんで いますか Minasan, doko ni sunde imasuka

Where do you live?

Take turns to be each of the people. Say what your name is and where you live.

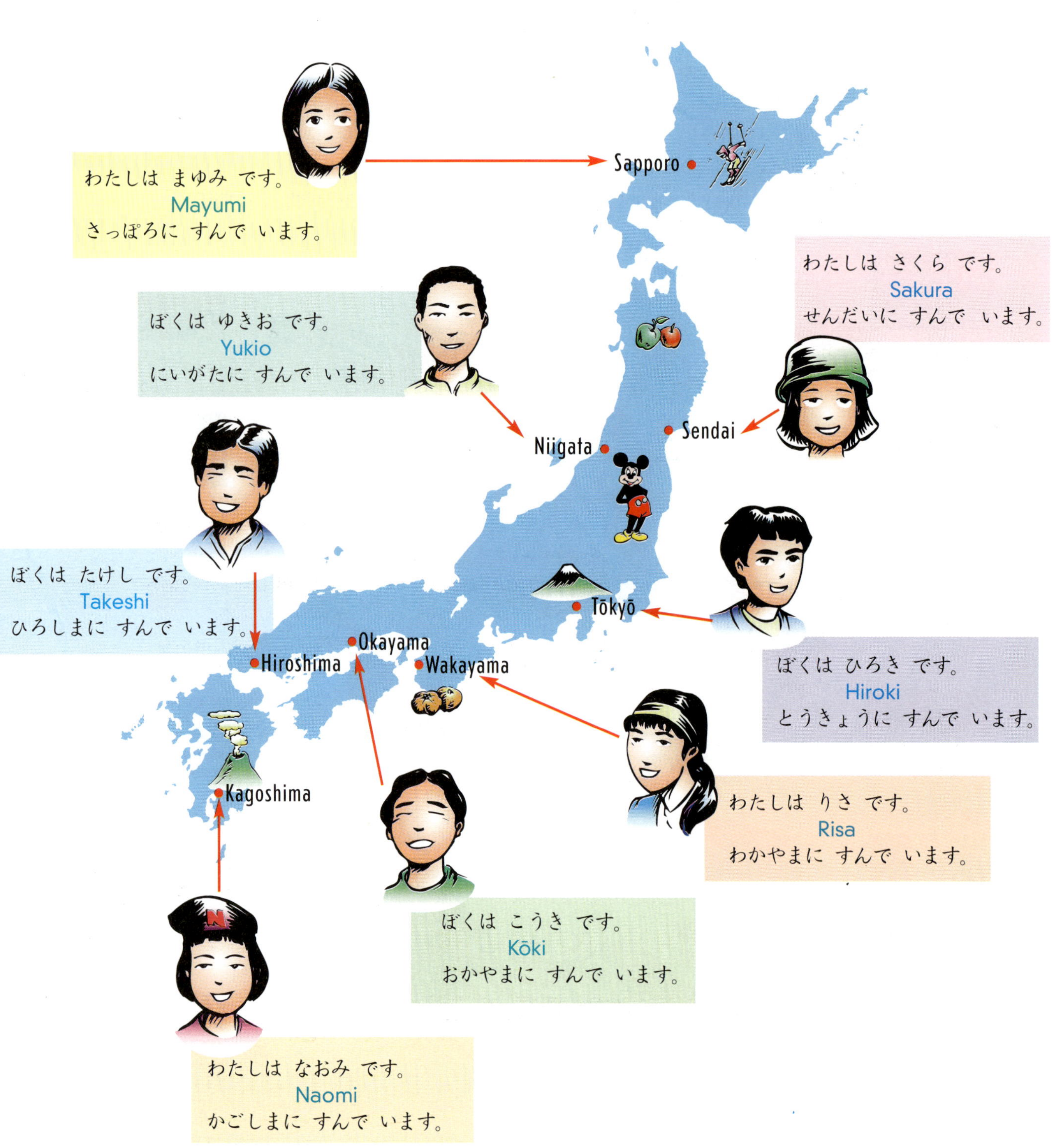

わたしは まゆみ です。
Mayumi
さっぽろに すんで います。
Sapporo
わたしは さくら です。
Sakura
せんだいに すんで います。
ぼくは ゆきお です。
Yukio
にいがたに すんで います。
Niigata
Sendai
ぼくは たけし です。
Takeshi
ひろしまに すんで います。
Tōkyō
Hiroshima
Okayama
Wakayama
ぼくは ひろき です。
Hiroki
とうきょうに すんで います。
Kagoshima
わたしは りさ です。
Risa
わかやまに すんで います。
ぼくは こうき です。
Kōki
おかやまに すんで います。
わたしは なおみ です。
Naomi
かごしまに すんで います。

わかった Wakatta! I'VE GOT IT!

Asking where someone lives	どこ Doko	に ni	すんで います sunde imasu	か。 ka.	
Saying where you live	[Town/suburb]	に ni	すんで います。 sunde imasu.		
Asking for someone's country of birth	おくに Okuni	は wa	どこ doko	です desu	か。 ka.
Answering which country you come from			[Country]	です。	
Guessing nationality	[Country]	じん -jin	です desu	か。 ka.	
Saying your nationality	[Country]	じん -jin	です。 desu.		

べんきょう の こつ What's your secret? Benkyō no kotsu

Ken, how do you learn all these lists? You seem to know lots of countries, numbers and things. I can ask someone how old and what nationality they are, but I can't always understand the answer.

I write the new words on blank name cards. I put Japanese on one side and the English meaning on the other. I keep them in my pocket and whenever I have a few minutes, I look at the meaning and say the Japanese aloud or in my head. I put aside all the ones I can do and work on the ones I can't remember. I learn all new words like this, even in other subjects like science.

Some people punch holes in the cards and put them on a ring.

CHINESE PERSON
Chuugoku-jin
どこ
じん
PERSON

インフォ
Info
DID YOU KNOW?

About Japan

Compared to Australia, the total area of Japan is very small, covering only 377 835 square kilometres compared to Australia's 7 682 300 square kilometres. Most of Japan consists of rugged mountains and hilly country, on which it is impossible to build houses. As a result, 77% of the 125 million Japanese people are crowded together in cities built on the coastal plains.

Although the land mass of Australia is very large compared to Japan, and the population much smaller, 88% of Australians also live in cities on the coast.

Japanese cities are much more crowded than the cities of Australia. Land is in short supply and extremely expensive. Very few people have the luxury of living in spacious houses with gardens. In big cities such as Tōkyō, which has more than eight million people, many people live in apartment blocks. However, these are usually very conveniently located, close to shopping centres and stations. Some have children's playgrounds and shops on the ground floor.

Public parks and gardens such as the Meiji Park in Tōkyō are huge and very popular.

In smaller cities, more people are able to live in a house instead of an apartment. Gardens are small but well cared for and each household cleans the street area outside their own home. Shopkeepers also sweep the pavements outside their own shop and keep the area clean. Although Japanese cities are densely populated, they are generally clean and tidy.

Fewer people inhabit the villages and small towns in the beautiful inland valleys. Others live on small farms. Fewer still live on many of the 1000 small islands that dot the coast.

Some live in small fishing villages and towns along the rugged coast. These people live more tranquil lives, surrounded by the spectacular natural beauty of Japan. They are able to enjoy the changing moods of the mountains, volcanoes, lakes and rivers that surround their country homes. None of these country districts is far from a major city, though, and as most places are linked by fast rail services, most country folk can enjoy big city life whenever they feel like it.

Many city-dwellers were born in a country village or town, or have grandparents who still live there. These people consider that place as their *furusato* or home town. No matter how long they have lived in the city, they try to return to their *furusato* at least twice a year, to take part in the special festivals and celebrations.

The most popular times to visit one's *furusato* are during the *Obon* festival in August and the *Oshōgatsu* celebration at New Year.

Obon is a celebration in honor of departed ancestors. Huge, colourful floats lit with lanterns are pulled through the streets. Atop the floats, teams of dancers wearing kimonos demonstrate traditional *Obon* dances. Musicians play traditional music and massive drums are struck to keep the beat.

祈禱受付所

Oshōgatsu, or New Year, is the most important celebration of the year. Houses are spring-cleaned and special dishes are cooked in advance, so that no cooking is done on New Year's Day itself. The feast is served in lacquered boxes.

Everyone sends greeting cards to their friends, relatives and work colleagues. The post office delivers all the cards on the first of January. Everyone welcomes the steady streams of visitors and relatives. Children receive special gifts of money called *otoshidama* which are presented in attractively decorated envelopes.

あいさつ

Aisatsu

Greetings (II)

At home

おはよう。
Ohayō.
おはよう。
Ohayō.
ただいま。
Tadaima.
おかえり なさい。
Okaeri nasai.
ただいま。
Tadaima.
おかえり なさい。
Okaeri nasai.
いって きます。
Itte kimasu.
いって らっしゃい。
Itte rasshai.

Meeting in the morning …

Meeting in the afternoon …

Meeting in the evening …

Leaving …

At the judo academy

おはよう ございます。
Ohayō gozaimasu.
おはよう。
Ohayō.
こんにちは。
Konnichi wa.
こんにちは。
Konnichi wa.
こんばんは。
Konban wa.
こんばんは。
Konban wa.
さようなら。
Sayōnara.
じゃ、また。
Ja, mata.

Polite expressions at the table

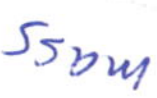

いただきます。
Itadakimasu.
ごちそうさま。
Gochisōsama.

せつめい コーナー
Setsumei koonaa

Explanation corner

Before you eat

We use a lot of set expressions in daily life. Before eating anything we always say, いただきます **itadakimasu**. This means *I gratefully receive this*. It is a kind of grace.

After eating

After eating we say, ごちそうさま **gochisōsama**. This means *It was very nice food*.

We don't think about what these expressions mean, we just say them. I heard that *Goodbye* used to be *God be with you*, but no one thinks about the original meaning any more. Is that true? Can you think of any others? How about *How do you do?*

Goodbye

We only say さようなら **sayōnara** when leaving someone for a long time or in formal situations. When we leave the house, we always say, casually, いってきます **itte kimasu**. This means *I'm going and I'm coming back*. The person who is left in the house says, いってらっしゃい **itte rasshai**. This means *Go and welcome back*.

I'm back

When we come home we always say, ただいま **tadaima**. This just means *Now (I'm back)*. The person inside says, おかえり なさい **okaeri nasai**. This means *Welcome home*.

Again, we don't think about the basic meaning of these greetings; we just say them. If you ever go for a homestay with a Japanese family you should use these expressions too.

できますか
Dekimasuka
CAN YOU DO IT?

AB p. 19

1 Listen to the conversations and tick the picture that fits the greetings you hear.

a
b
c
d
e
f

2 When should you say these expressions?
Draw a line from the expressions to the correct situation.

ごちそうさま Gochisōsama	いって らっしゃい Itte rasshai	いただきます Itadakimasu	おかえり なさい Okaeri-nasai	いって きます Itte kimasu	ただいま Tadaima

わかった！ Wakatta! I'VE GOT IT!

Polite table manners	
Before eating food say	いただきます Itadakimasu
After eating food say	ごちそうさま Gochisōsama

Returning home	
If you are returning home say	ただいま Tadaima
If you are the one inside say	おかえり　なさい Okaeri nasai

Saying goodbye to people who live with you	
If you are leaving say	いって　きます Itte kimasu
If you are staying say	いって　らっしゃい Itte rasshai

なに？　なに？ Nani? Nani?

What are they saying?

ごちそうさま。

いただきます。

ひらがな

Hiragana

に	ま	し (じ)	せ (ぜ)
ni	ma	shi (ji)	se (ze)
に for Nihon	ま for mask	し for shield	せ for send a parcel

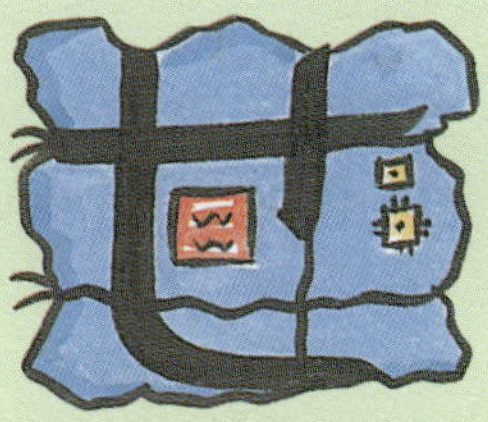

な	と (ど)	か (が)
na	to (do)	ka (ga)
な for nap	と for top	か for kangaroo

ん	わ	ら	や	ま	は	な	た	さ	か	あ
		り		み	ひ	に	ち	し	き	い
		る	ゆ	む	ふ	ぬ	つ	す	く	う
		れ		め	へ	ね	て	せ	け	え
	を	ろ	よ	も	ほ	の	と	そ	こ	お

ひらがな れんしゅう

Hiragana renshuu

AB pp. 21–25

Hiragana exercises

1 Write the correct hiragana in the squares.

	ん	せ	い	、		こ		す	ん	で	い		す		。

Kyanbera	に		ん		い	ま		。

Naomi		ん	は	Oosutoraria		ん	で		。

Ken	く		は		ん	さ	い		す		。

ぼ			14	さ			す	。

Kanada	じ		で		。

2 Write the missing hiragana on the soccer balls to kick the soccer ball to the goal!

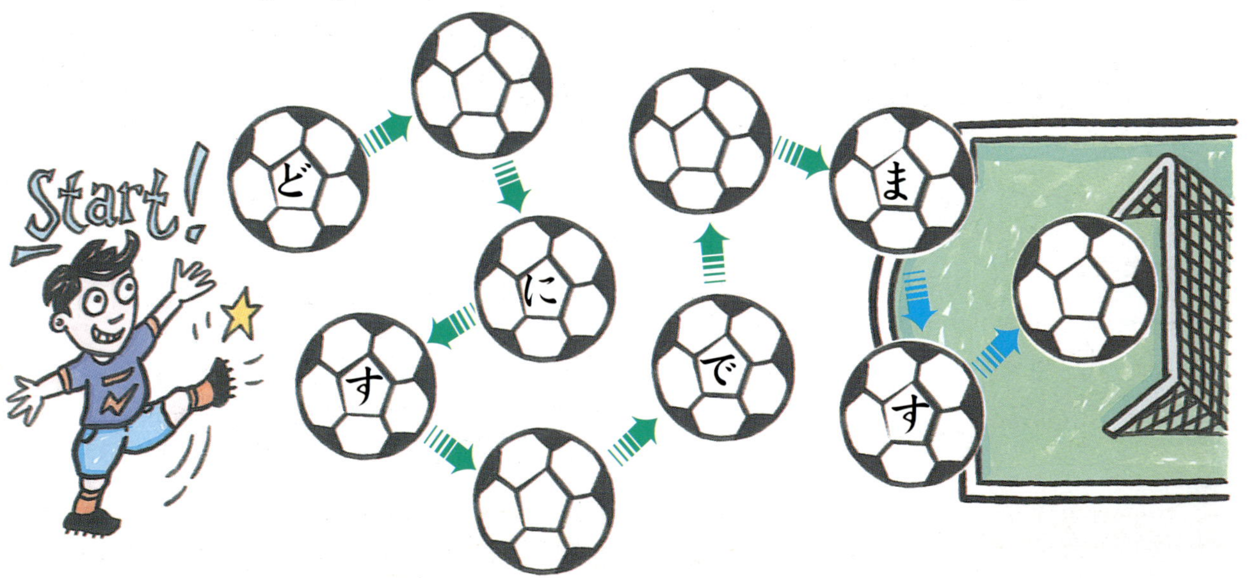
Start!
ど
に
す
で
ま
す

てんせい

こけこっこう！

にほん じん
ですか。
はい。てんせい です。
どうぞ よろしく。

いただきます！
てんせいくん
どこに すんで
いますか。

うちゅうに すんで
います。

ああ、そう ですか。
うちゅう
STATION

ごちそうさま！

いって きます！
いって
らっしゃい！
あ、おべんと
う！
ありがとう！

うちゅう 2 km

AB pp. 26–27

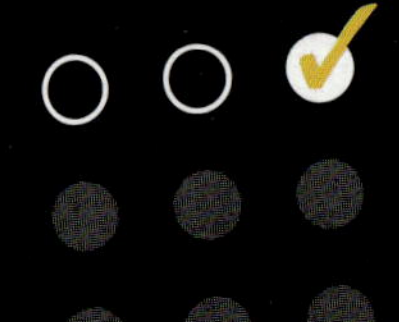

チェックしましょう！ Chekku shimashō!

Let's check!

Suffixes	
〜じん	~ person

Question words	
どこ	where?

Verb	
すんで　います	live, am living

Expressions	
ああ、そう ですか Aa, sō desuka	Really? Is that so?
いただきます Itadakimasu	Say this before eating
おくに okuni	Your country
ごちそうさま Gochisōsama	Say this after eating
そう です Sō desu	That's right

Greetings	
いって きます Itte kimasu	'Bye (the speaker is leaving)
いって らっしゃい Itte rasshai	'Bye (the speaker is staying)
おかえり なさい Okaeri nasai	Welcome home
じゃ、また Ja, mata	See you again
ただいま Tadaima	I'm home now

Some nationalities	
アメリカ じん Amerika-jin	American person
インドネシア じん Indoneshia-jin	Indonesian person
オーストラリア じん Oosutoraria-jin	Australian person
カナダ じん Kanada-jin	Canadian person
ちゅうごく じん Chuugoku-jin	Chinese person
ドイツ じん Doitsu-jin	German person
にほん じん Nihon-jin	Japanese person
ニュージーランド じん Nyuujiirando-jin	New Zealander

I can:

- say where I live
- ask where others live
- say my nationality and ask about others' nationality
- keep the conversation going
- say goodbye three more ways
- say the correct things at mealtimes
- say I'm home
- read and write どこに　すんで　いますか。
- ... and ぼくも／わたしも Oosutoraria じん　です。

1
2
3
4
5
6
7
8
9

part 2

Gakkō

がっこう

School

At the end of Part 2 you will be able to:

- say what school grade you are in
- ask what grade someone is in
- understand the Japanese school system
- explain your school timetable
- say what your favourite subjects are
- say what your favourite food is
- follow classroom instructions
- read and write more sentences in hiragana.

Unit 4

なん ねんせい ですか

Nan nensei desuka

What grade are you in?

1

Isn't that boy new?

Yeah, he looks lost.

Is he Japanese?

Let's go and talk to him in Japanese!

2

おなまえは？
Onamae wa?

まさし です。
Masashi desu.

3

なん ねんせい ですか。
Nan-nensei desuka.

7ねんせい です。
Nana-nensei desu.

4

ぼくは ケン です。
Boku wa **Ken** desu.

わたしは ニッキー です。
Watashi wa **Nikkii** desu.
どうぞ よろしく。
Dōzo yoroshiku.

わたしも 7ねんせい です。
Watashi mo nana-nensei desu.

5

あのう、1じかんめは なん ですか。
Anō, ichi-jikan-me wa nan desuka.

すうがく です。
Suugaku desu.

6

ええ？
Ee?

7
すきな　かもくは　なん　ですか。
Sukina kamoku wa nan desuka.
たいいく　です。
Taiiku desu.
たいいくは
Taiiku wa
5じかんめ　です。
go-jikan-me desu.
6じかんめは
Roku-jikan-me wa
えいご　です。
Eigo desu.
8
ニッキーさん、すきな　かもくは　なん　ですか。
Nikkii-san, sukina kamoku wa nan desuka.
びじゅつ　です。
Bijutsu desu.
びじゅつは　3じかんめと　4じかんめ　です。
Bijutsu wa san-jikan-me to yo-jikan-me desu.
9
2じかんめは
Ni-jikan-me wa
なん　ですか。
nan desuka.
ええっと、2じかんめも
Eetto, ni-jikan-me mo
すうがく　です。
suugaku desu.
10
1じかんめと　2じかんめは　すうがく...
Ichi-jikan-me to ni-jikan-me wa suugaku ...

できますか
Dekimasuka
CAN YOU DO IT?

Can you find out ...

* what *nensei* means?
* what *jikan-me* means?
* what subject Masashi likes/dislikes?
* Masashi's schedule for today?

せつめい コーナー Setsumei koonaa

Explanation corner

How do I ask what grade someone is in?

To find out what grade someone is in, just say あのう、なん ねんせい ですか。**Anō, nan-nensei desuka.** あのう **Anō** is a bit like *Excuse me*.

To answer, just put the number of the grade you are in before ねんせい **nensei**.

For example, if you are in grade 6 you say, ろく ねんせい です。**Roku-nensei desu.** There is only one thing more to remember: you should say よ ねんせい **yo-nensei** for grade 4 and *not* よん ねんせい **yon-nensei**.

If you are talking to a Japanese person who does not know your school system, you will have to convert your grade to the Japanese system or they will not understand you. You will find a full explanation on page 65.

How do I say what period a subject is?

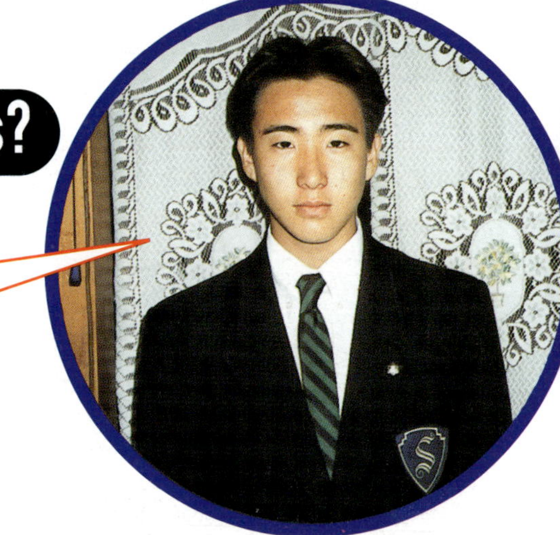

To say what period a subject is, use the word じかん **jikan** plus め **me**. The suffix め **me** changes a cardinal number (one, two etc) to an ordinal number (first, second etc).

For example, if you want to say that Japanese is first period you say, にほんごは 1じかんめ です。**Nihongo wa ichi-jikan-me desu.**

To say that first period is Japanese you say, 1じかんめは にほんご です。**Ichi-jikan-me wa Nihongo desu.**

By the way, you are learning にほんご **Nihongo** which is the word for Japanese language. In Japanese schools, the subject Japanese is called こくご **kokugo**.

WHAT A USEFUL EXPRESSION!

ええっと
eetto

This means *Um … let me see.* Use it when you are thinking of the answer.

Particles

5じかんめ と 6じかんめ
Go-jikan-me to roku-jikan me

The word と **to** in たいいくは 5じかんめと 6じかんめ です。**Taiiku wa go-jikan-me to roku-jikan-me desu** is another particle. Like the particle に **ni** it has a number of meanings. You will learn the other meanings later. This と only occurs between nouns and means *and*, so this sentence means *Phys. Ed is in period 5 and period 6*.

You
と
to
I

Asking what grade someone is in

Saying what grade you are in

なん ねんせい ですか。
Nan-nensei desuka.
8ねんせい です。
Hachi-nensei desu.
7ねんせい です。
Nana-nensei desu.
9ねんせい です。
Kyuu-nensei desu.

Asking about the timetable

Explaining the timetable

1じかんめは なん ですか。
Ichi-jikan-me wa nan desuka.
じかんわり
1じかんめは すうがく です。
Ichi-jikan-me wa suugaku desu.
たいいくは なん じかんめ ですか
Taiiku wa nan-jikan-me desuka.
たいいくは 5じかんめ と 6じかんめ です。
Taiiku wa go-jikan-me to roku-jikan-me desu.

かもく

Kamoku

School subjects in Japan

しゃかい
Shakai
ぎじゅつ かてい
Gijutsu katei
びじゅつ
Bijutsu
おんがく
Ongaku
すうがく
Suugaku
こくご
Kokugo
日本人
わたしは
えいご
Eigo
This is
They are
That is
たいいく
Taiiku
りか
Rika

できますか
Dekimasuka
CAN YOU DO IT?

Using the information on this page, prepare the timetable at your school in Japanese for a new Japanese student. If you need to find out the words for other subjects, ask your teacher.

AB pp. 28, 29

できますか Dekimasuka CAN YOU DO IT?

1 What grade is Mika in?

Take turns with a partner. Kitsune decides which grade Mika is in and secretly writes down the grade in the box under the picture.

Tanuki must find out which grade she is in by asking questions.

Kitsune can only answer はい Hai or いいえ Iie. *For example:*

Tanuki: みかさんは 1ねんせい ですか。Mika-san wa ichi-nensei desuka.

Kitsune: いいえ。Iie.

A maximum of five questions can be asked. The fewer the questions Tanuki needs to guess, the higher the score.

Use this table to keep score.

Question	1st	2nd	3rd	4th	5th
Points	10	8	6	4	2

______ ねんせい nensei

2 Which class do they belong to?

4じかんめは Yo-jikan-me wa なん ですか。nan desuka.

じかんわり Timetable Jikanwari

	A ぐみ gumi	B ぐみ	C ぐみ
1	りか Rika	れきし Rekishi	すうがく Suugaku
2	こくご Kokugo	すうがく Suugaku	りか Rika
3	びじゅつ Bijutsu	おんがく Ongaku	たいいく Taiiku
4	れきし Rekishi	ちり Chiri	こくご Kokugo
5	えいご Eigo	こくご Kokugo	ちり Chiri
6	すうがく Suugaku	えいご Eigo	びじゅつ Bijutsu

こくご です。Kokugo desu.

Keiko

5じかんめは Go-jikan-me wa なん ですか。nan desuka.

えいご です。Eigo desu.

Yumi

2じかんめは なん ですか。Ni-jikan-me wa nan desuka.

すうがく です。Suugaku desu.

Hiro

かもく ビンゴ・ゲーム

Kamoku bingo

えいご
English
すうがく
Maths
りか
Science
しゃかい
Social Science
びじゅつ
Art
にほんご
Japanese
たいいく
Physical Education
おんがく
Music
ぎじゅつかてい
Manual Arts
りか
Science
びじゅつ
Art
えいご
English
れきし
History
すうがく
Maths
にほんご
Japanese
ちり
Geography

Rules

Game 1

Play in threes. Kitsune must cross out all the subjects on the diagonal cross. Tanuki must cross out the top line and the bottom line. (You can vary this, as long as you each have the same number of subjects.) The caller makes a list of all the subjects on the page and cuts the list into strips with one word on each strip. The caller randomly selects a strip and calls out the subject in Japanese. The first person to cross out all their words calls out *Bingo*.

Game 2

Play in groups. Your teacher allocates a different line for each group and calls out the subjects. The first group to cross out all their subjects and say *Bingo* is the winning group.

AB p. 28

インフォ
Info
DID YOU KNOW?

School grades in Japan

ようちえん Kindergarten

ようちえん
Yōchien

QUIZ

Here are the Jones children. What grade would they be in the Japanese system?

1 Jason: grade 12
2 Sharon: grade 9
3 Kim: grade 7
4 Ben: grade 3

しょうがっこう Primary school Shōgakkō

Grade at home: 1, 2, 3, 4, 5, 6

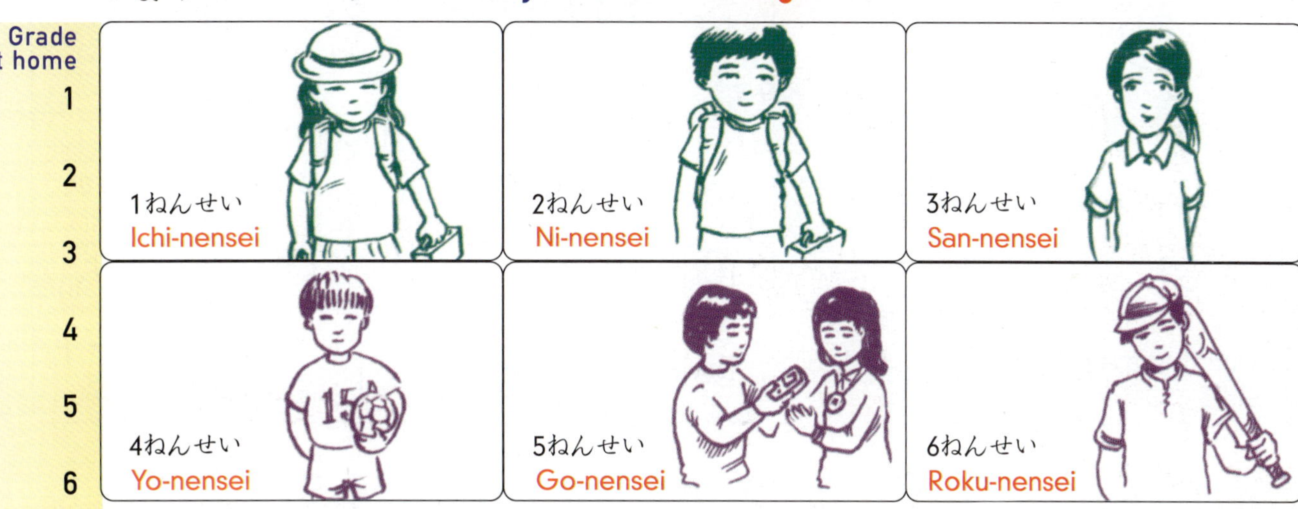

Grade at home			
1, 2, 3	1ねんせい Ichi-nensei	2ねんせい Ni-nensei	3ねんせい San-nensei
4, 5, 6	4ねんせい Yo-nensei	5ねんせい Go-nensei	6ねんせい Roku-nensei

ちゅうがっこう Junior high school Chuugakkō

Grade at home			
7, 8, 9	ちゅうがく 1ねんせい Ichi-nensei	ちゅうがく 2ねんせい Ni-nensei	ちゅうがく 3ねんせい San-nensei

こうこう Senior high school Kōkō

Grade at home			
10, 11, 12	こうこう 1ねんせい Ichi-nensei	こうこう 2ねんせい Ni-nensei	こうこう 3ねんせい San-nensei

わかった！ Wakatta! I'VE GOT IT!

Asking what grade someone is in	なん Nan	ねんせい nensei	です desu	か。 ka.				
Saying what grade you are in (Grade 1–12 system)	1–12	ねんせい nensei	です。 desu.					
Saying what grade you are, in Japan	(Primary)	しょうがっこう Shōgakkō	1–6	ねんせい nensei	です。 desu.			
	(Junior high)	ちゅうがく Chuugakkō	1–3	ねんせい nensei	です。 desu.			
	(Senior high)	こうこう Kōkō	1–3	ねんせい nensei	です。 desu.			
Asking what subject is in periods 1–8	1–8	じかんめ jikan-me	は wa	なん nan	です desu	か。 ka.		
Saying what subject is in periods 1–8	1–8	じかんめ jikan-me	は wa	[subject]	です。 desu.			
Asking what period a subject is	[Subject]	は wa	なん nan	じかんめ jikan-me	ですか。 desuka.			
Saying that a subject is in period 1	[Subject]	は wa	1 ichi	じかんめ jikan-me	です。 desu.			
Saying that a subject is in period 1 and 2	[Subject]	は wa	1 ichi	じかんめ jikan-me	と to	2 ni	じかんめ jikan-me	です。 desu.

べんきょう の こつ What's your secret
Benkyō no kotsu

Johnny, you always do so well in class tests. How do you remember so much?

Look, I used to panic before tests and try to learn everything the night before. Now, I try to be organised. I keep a special notebook for Japanese divided into different sections. I have pages for vocabulary divided into topics. I only put one topic per page so that I can keep on adding to it as I learn new words. I have a separate section for sentences and another section for expressions.

I read them through several times a week. It doesn't take very long, and I can revise from my notes instead of reading the Course Book again. I do the same for other subjects too.

Being organised gives me more time to have fun as well. Best of all, I don't panic any more!

インフォ
Info
DID YOU KNOW?

Schooling in Japan

Compulsory schooling

Schooling in Japan is compulsory for nine years, that is the six years of *shōgakkō* (primary) and the three years of *chuugakkō* (junior high). To get into *kōkō* (senior high), students have to pass an entrance examination. Different high schools set their own entrance examinations, the most popular setting the hardest examinations. Twelve-to-fourteen-year-old students usually have to study very hard to gain entry to one of the better high schools.

Once they have successfully entered their chosen high, they have to work even harder for the next hurdle: the university entrance exams. Many Japanese children attend a *juku* (a coaching college) after school hours to improve their chances of passing the tough examinations.

Keeping the school clean

All students in Japanese schools are responsible for keeping the school clean. They not only clean their own classrooms but also the hallways, labs, gyms and toilets. They work on a roster system. Schools set aside 15–20 minutes for cleaning up, as part of the daily routine. Even Grade 1 pupils have to take on the responsibility of cleaning their own areas. In this way, students learn to cooperate with each other and to take pride in the cleanliness of their school.

Most schools have an area close to the entrance for changing shoes. Students are expected to change their outside shoes for slippers or inside shoes. They place their outside shoes on shoe racks. This is what people do at home, too, which keeps the inside of buildings free of mud and dirt.

QUIZ

What do you know about Japanese schools?

1. How many years does kōkō last?
2. How many years does shōgakkō last?
3. How many years compulsory schooling are there?
4. What is a *juku*?
5. What is the word for junior high?
6. Who cleans a Japanese school?

すきな かもくは なん ですか
Sukina kamoku wa nan desuka?

What subjects do you like?

すきな かもくは なん ですか。
Sukina kamoku wa nan desuka.
しゃかい です。
Shakai desu.
ええっと、すきな かもくは りか です。
Eetto, sukina kamoku wa rika desu.
おんがく と びじゅつ です。
Ongaku to bijutsu desu.
たいいく と にほんご と えいご です。
Taiiku to Nihongo to Eigo desu.
すきな かもくは？
Sukina kamoku wa?
ぎじゅつかてい です。
Gijutsu katei desu.
すうがく と りか です。
Suugaku to rika desu.
ドイツご と にほんご です。
Doitsugo to Nihongo desu.
ちり と れきし です。
Chiri to rekishi desu.
フランスごと にほんご です。
Furansugo to Nihongo desu.

せつめい コーナー
Setsumei koonaa?

Explanation corner

How do I ask what someone's favourite subjects are?

To ask *What is your favourite subject?* say, すきな かもくは なん ですか **Sukina kamoku wa nan desuka.** すきな **sukina** means *favourite*. かもく **kamoku** means *school subject*.

Notice that there is no word for *your* in this sentence. We don't use personal pronouns much. We prefer to use people's names. Talking face-to-face with someone, though, it isn't necessary to use their name.

化学IB

To answer すきな かもくは なん ですか **Sukina kamoku wa nan desuka,** just say the name of the subject and add です。My favourite subject is science so I would answer, りか です **Rika desu**.

If you have more than one favourite subject use と **to** between the subjects. For example, ちり と りか です **Chiri to rika desu.**

To say the name of a country's language is very easy. Just say the name of the country and add ご **go.** Can you guess what these languages are?

- フランスご Furansu-go
- ドイツご Doitsu-go
- インドネシアご Indoneshia-go
- イタリアご Itaria-go
- ちゅうごくご Chuugoku-go

In the case of English it is えいご **Eigo**, *not* イギリスご **Igirisu-go.** This is because the formal word for England is えいこく **Eikoku.**

AB p. 30

できますか Dekimasuka CAN YOU DO IT?

1 Listen to a group of students talking and connect their names to their favourite subjects.

1	Akira	a	Social Studies
2	Hiro	b	English
3	Nicki	c	Art
4	Ken	d	Music
5	Emma	e	Phys. Ed. (PE)
6	Naomi	f	Maths

2 Listen to a new exchange student telling you about himself. Fill in the gaps in the information sheet.

Information Sheet

ぼくは＿＿＿＿＿です。

＿＿＿ねん＿＿＿です。

＿＿＿さい＿＿＿。

かごしまに＿＿＿ ＿＿＿。

すきな＿＿＿＿＿は

しゃ＿＿＿と＿＿＿＿です。

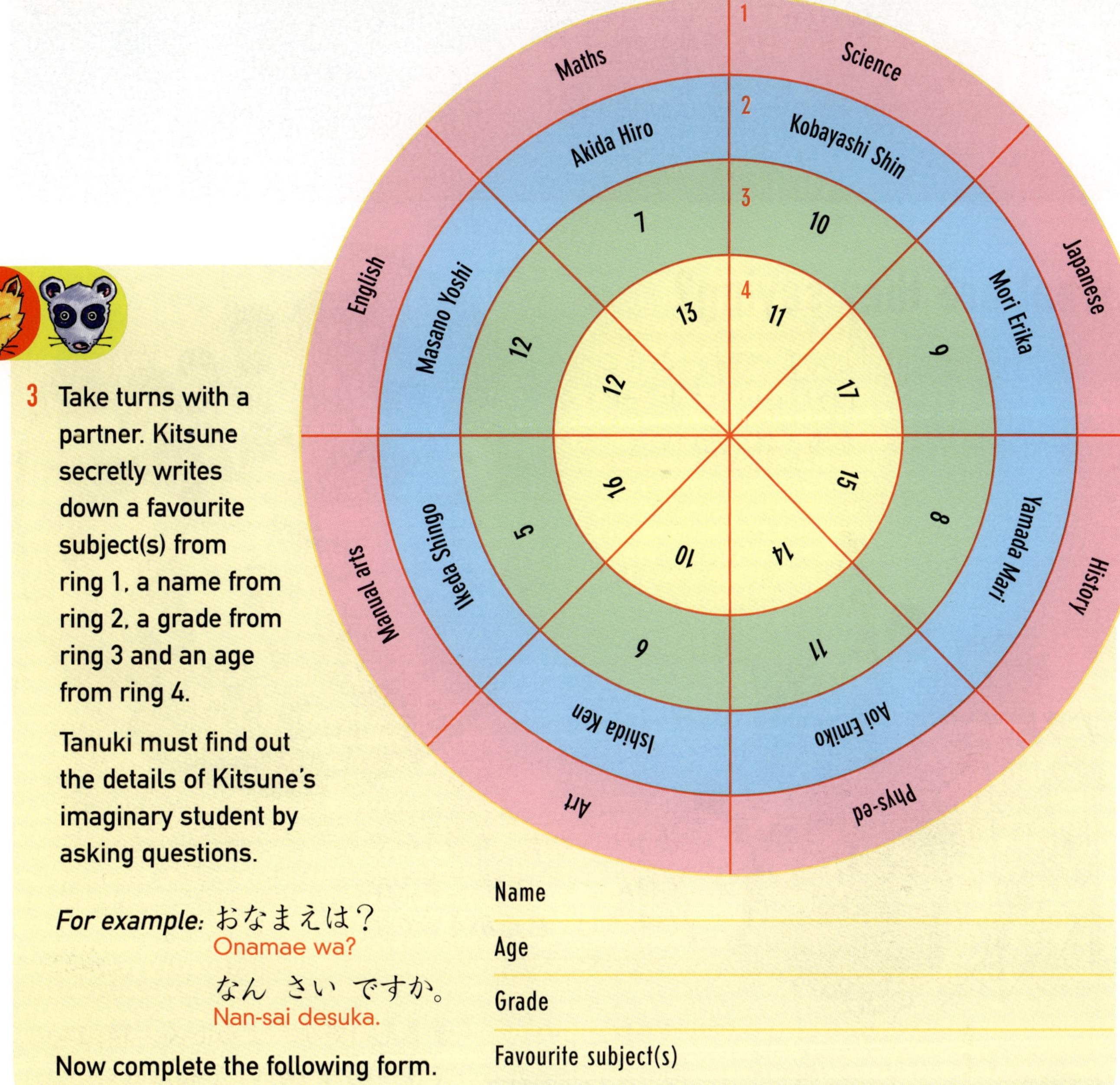

1
Science
Japanese
History
Phys-ed
Art
Manual arts
English
Maths
2
Kobayashi Shin
Mori Erika
Yamada Mari
Aoi Emiko
Ishida Ken
Ikeda Shingo
Masano Yoshi
Akida Hiro
3
10
9
8
11
9
5
12
7
4
11
17
15
14
10
16
12
13

3 Take turns with a partner. Kitsune secretly writes down a favourite subject(s) from ring 1, a name from ring 2, a grade from ring 3 and an age from ring 4.

Tanuki must find out the details of Kitsune's imaginary student by asking questions.

For example: おなまえは？
Onamae wa?
なん さい ですか。
Nan-sai desuka.

Now complete the following form.

Name ______________________

Age ______________________

Grade ______________________

Favourite subject(s) ______________________

Hiragana puzzles

1 Circle the odd sounds.
a たかしさ
b もほとい
c てすけせ

2 What are the jumbled words?
a しわた
b いせんせ
c いんせね
d いさんな
e まいすんすで

3 What are the missing syllables?
a でん＿ばんご＿は？
b な＿さい＿すか。
c どこ＿すんで＿ます＿。

4 What's the subject? Match the subject and its name in hiragana.

れきし	おんがく	りか	たいいく	ちり	すうがく	にほんご	えいご
Japanese	Maths	English	History	Science	Music	Phys. Ed.	Geography

なに？ なに？

Nani? Nani?

What are they saying?

しんご です。こうこう
1ねんせい です。すきな
かもくは たいいく です。

SEIFU

ゆかり です。ちゅうがく
2ねんせい です。すきな
かもくは おんがく です。

まさし です。よろしく。14 さい
です。ちゅうがく 2ねんせい
です。かごしまに すんで います。

こんにちは。ともき です。すきな
かもくは ぎじゅつかてい です。

わかった！ Wakatta! I'VE GOT IT!

Asking someone's favourite subject	すきな Sukina	かもく kamoku	は wa	なん nan	です desu	か。 ka.	
Saying what your favourite subject is	すきな Sukina	かもく kamoku	は wa	[subject] [subject]	です。 desu.		
Saying what your favourite subjects are	すきな Sukina	かもく kamoku	は wa	[subject] [subject]	と to	[subject] [subject]	です。 desu.
Saying a country's language	[Country]ご go						

あそびましょう Asobimashō

Origami かぶと Kabuto

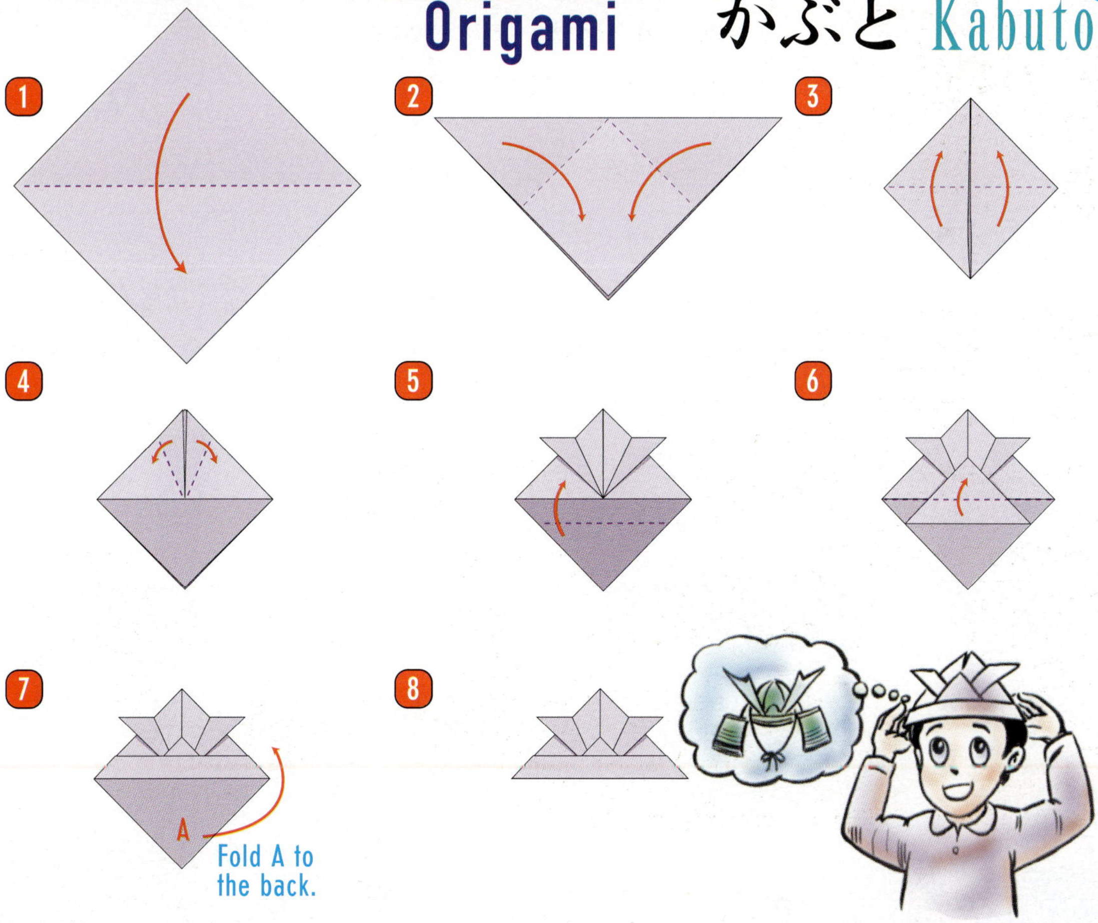

1

2

3

4

5

6

7

Fold A to the back.

8

Here is the helmet worn by Samurai warriors.

ひらがな Hiragana

き ぎ	め	ね	え
ki gi	me	ne	e
き	め	ね	え
き for kicking	め for mending the mesh	ね for nest	え for elbow
か が	お	り	れ
ka ga	o	ri	re
か	お	り	れ
か for kangaroo	お for oasis	り for ribbon	れ for rest

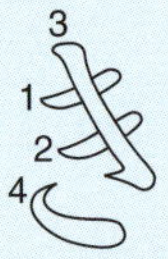

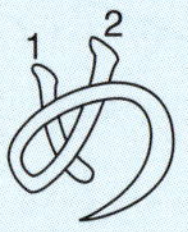

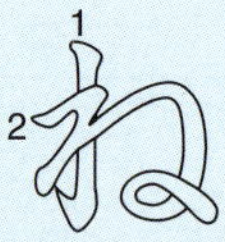

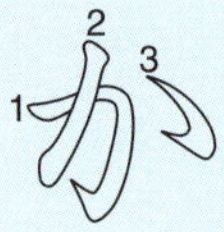

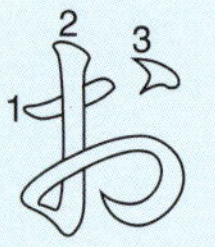

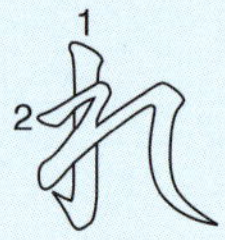

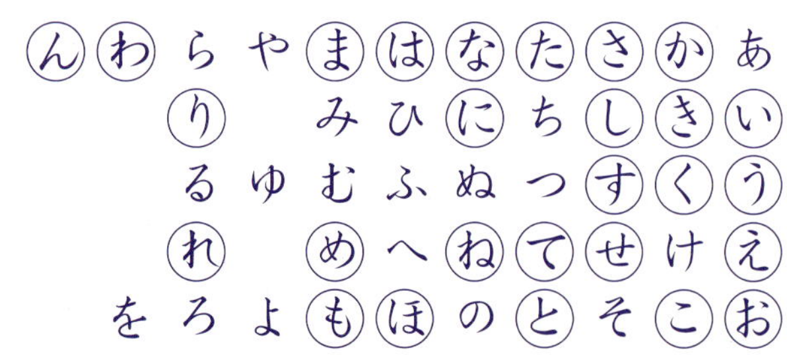

ん わ ら や ま は な た さ か あ
り み ひ に ち し き い
る ゆ む ふ ぬ つ す く う
れ め へ ね て せ け え
を ろ よ も ほ の と そ こ お

ひらがな れんしゅう

Hiragana renshuu

AB pp. 31-33

1 Write the correct hiragana in the squares.

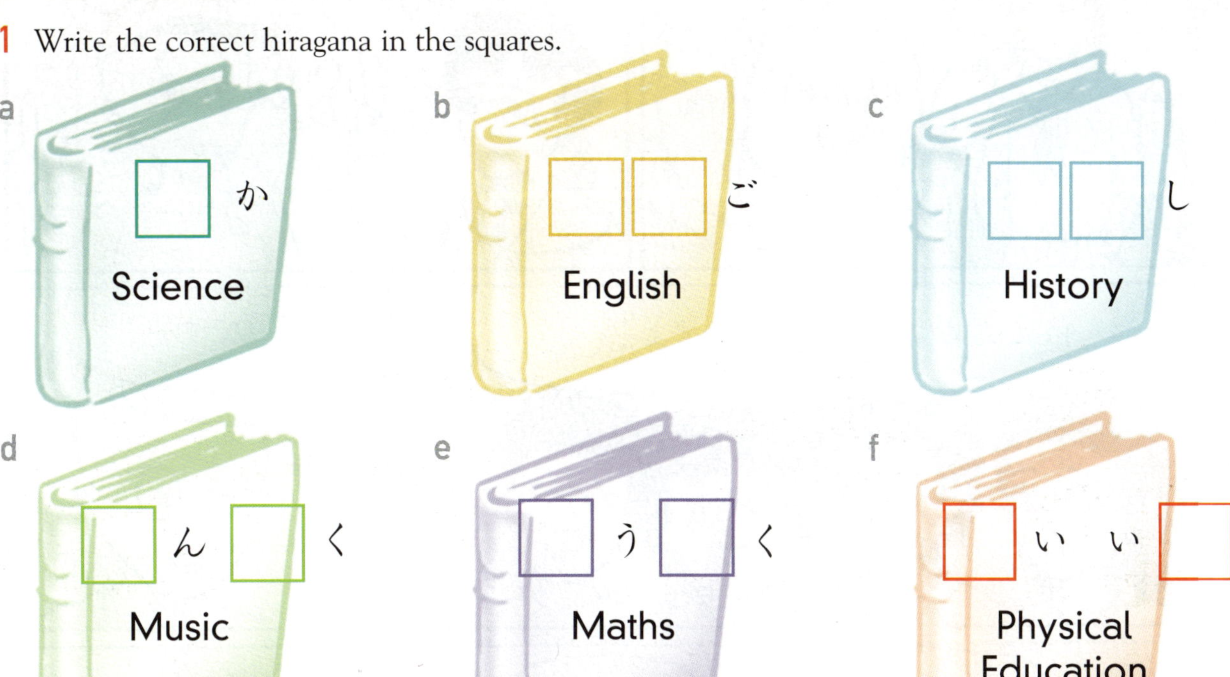
a
□か
Science
b
□□ご
English
c
□□し
History
d
□ん□く
Music
e
□う□く
Maths
f
□いい□
Physical Education

2 Answer the questions by filling in the blanks with hiragana and numerals.

a なん　ねんせい　ですか。

________________ です。

b すきな　かもくは　なん　ですか。

________________ です。(or ________________ と ________________ です。)

c すうがくは　なん　じかんめ　ですか。

________________ です。(or ________________ と ________________ です。)

d たいいくは　なん　じかんめ　ですか。

________________ です。(or ________________ と ________________ です。)

てんせい

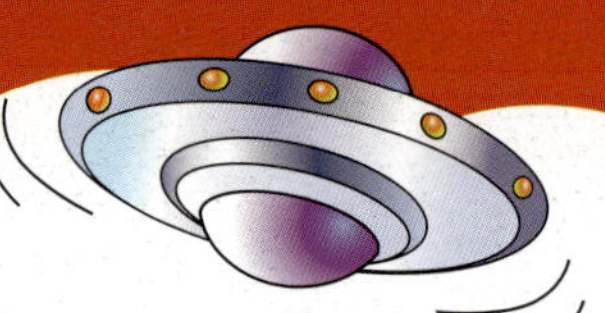

なん　ねんせい　ですか。
8ねんせい　です。

すきな　かもくは　なん　ですか。
ええっと、すうがく　です！

1じかんめは　すうがく　ですよ！

そう　ですか！

できますか。
はい、せんせい。

2じかんめは　なん　ですか。
こくご　です。

こくご⁉

ぼく、こくごは　ちょっと…

AB p. 34-35

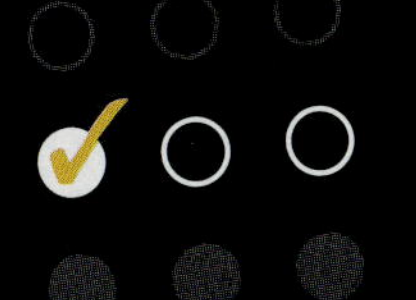

チェックしましょう
Chekku shimashō!

Let's check!

Suffixes

~ねんせい	~grade in school
~じかん	~(school) period, hour
~め	~ordinal number

Expressions

あのう Anō ...	Um ... (excuse me)
ええっと... Eetto ...	Um ... let me see ...

Adjective

すきな	favourite

The Japanese school system

しょうがっこう shōgakkō	primary school
ちゅうがっこう chuugakkō	junior high school
こうこう kōkō	senior high school

Some school subjects

えいご	English
おんがく	Music
こくご	Japanese language (in Japan)
ぎじゅつかてい Gijutsu katei	Design and Technology
すうがく	Maths
しゃかい Shakai	Social Studies
たいいく	Physical Education
ちり Chiri	Geography
にほんご	Japanese (as a second language)
びじゅつ Bijutsu	Art
りか	Science
れきし	History

School words

がっこう	school
かもく	subject
Aぐみ A gumi	Class A
じかんわり jikanwari	timetable

I can:

- ask what grade someone is in and say what grade I am in
- ask at what period three subjects are and say what period three more subjects are
- ask what someone's favourite subject is
- convert grades to the Japanese system
- say the name of four languages

read and write ...

- なん ねんせい ですか。
- すきな かもくは なん ですか。
- 1じかんめは なん ですか。
- おんがく、すうがく、たいいく、りか、こくご、えいご、れきし

9
8
7
6
5
4
3
2
1

Unit 5

りかは おもしろい です

Rika wa omoshiroi desu

Science is interesting

1 Lunch break

ひろくん、すきな かもくは なん ですか。
Hiro-kun, sukina kamoku wa nan desuka.

りか です。
Rika desu.

2

りかは やさしい ですか。
Rika wa yasashii desuka.

いいえ、むずかしい です。
Iie, muzukashii desu.

3

でも、おもしろい です。
Demo omoshiroi desu.

4

カレンさんは？
Karen-san wa?

5

おんがく です。おんがくは たのしい です。
Ongaku desu. Ongaku wa tanoshii desu.

6

そう ですね びじゅつも たのしい です。
Sō desu ne. Bijutsu mo tanoshii desu.

7
ニッキーさん、ランチは　なん　ですか。
Nikkii-san, ranchi wa nan desuka.
ベジマイト
Bejimaito
サンドイッチ　です。
sandoitchi desu.
8
どうぞ！
Dōzo!
いいえ、ベジマイトは
Iie, bejimaito wa
ちょっと…
chotto …
9
ひろくん、ランチは
Hiro-kun, ranchi wa
なん　ですか。
nan desuka.
おべんとう　です。
Obentō desu.
10
11
おいしい　ですか。
Oishii desuka.
はい。おいしい
Hai. Oishii
ですよ。
desu yo.
12
どうぞ！
Dōzo!
13
… ありがとう …
… Arigatō …
14
おいしい！
Oishii!

できますか
Dekimasuka
CAN YOU DO IT?

Can you find out …

- ✱ what Hiro's favourite subject is?
- ✱ why he likes the subject?
- ✱ what Karen's favourite subject is?
- ✱ why she likes the subject?
- ✱ the word meaning *delicious*?
- ✱ the expression for offering some food.

せつめい コーナー
Setsumei koonaa

Explanation corner

How do I say Phys. Ed. is fun?

To make comments about things such as school subjects is really easy. You just need to learn some adjectives to describe them. You say the topic followed by は **wa** and then say the adjective plus です **desu.** To say *Phys. Ed. is fun* you say, たいいくは　たのしい　です。**Taiiku wa tanoshii desu.**

To make a question just add か **ka,** as in たいいくは　たのしい　ですか。**Taiiku wa tanoshii desuka.**

To answer the question, you can agree, as in はい、たのしい　です。**Hai, tanoshii desu** or disagree by saying いいえ plus an adjective that expresses what you really think, as in いいえ、つまらない　です。**Iie, tsumaranai desu.**

By the way, to say two contrasting things about something, link them together with でも **demo** which means *but* or *however*. For example, to express the idea, *Science is difficult, but it is interesting*, you can say, りかは　むずかしい　です。でも、おもしろい　です。**Rika wa muzukashii desu. Demo, omoshiroi desu.**

WHAT A USEFUL EXPRESSION!

そう　ですね。
Sō desu ne.

Use it when you agree with what the other person is saying. It means *That's right isn't it?* Japanese use it very often where you might say *Uh huh, Mmm* or just nod.

Particles

たのしい ですよ
Tanoshi desu yo

The little word よ **yo** is a special particle. It always comes at the end of a sentence. Use it when you are asserting something. It is a bit like saying *I'm telling you*. It would be better to avoid using it to teachers and adults. You might sound too assertive.

Sentence
よ
yo
I'm telling you.

Asking if a subject is easy / Agreeing / Disagreeing

りかは やさしい ですか。
Rika wa yasashii desuka.
はい、やさしい です。
Hai, yasashii desu.
いいえ、むずかしい です。
Iie, muzukashii desu.
A
D

Asserting that a subject is enjoyable ... or boring

たいいくは たのしい ですよ。
Taiiku wa tanoshii desu yo.
たいいくは つまらない ですよ。
Taiiku wa tsumaranai desu yo.

Making contrasting comments

すうがくは むずかしい です。
Suugaku wa muzukashii desu.
でも、おもしろい です。
Demo, omoshiroi desu.
たなか せんせいは きびしい です。
Tanaka-sensei wa kibishii desu.
でも、おもしろい です。
Demo, omoshiroi desu.

けいようし

Keiyōshi

Adjectives

Describing school subjects

2 × 3 =
10 − 5 =

やさしい！
Yasashii!

むずかしい ...
Muzukashii ...

おもしろい。
Omoshiroi.

つまらない。
Tsumaranai.

たのしい！
Tanoshii!

まあまあ ...
Maamaa ...

Describing teachers

Forgot your book? Lunchtime detention! Extra homework!
きびしい ...
Kibishii ...
Forgot your book? Be careful next time. Here. Use mine.
やさしい！
Yasashii!
If you need my help, ask me anytime.
しんせつ。
Shinsetsu.
おもしろい。
Omoshiroi.

できますか Dekimasuka CAN YOU DO IT?

1 Akiko is talking about her school subjects. How does she feel about them?

Subject	Her opinion

2 Kitsune chooses a favourite subject from among the books below. Tanuki must guess which is Kitsune's favourite subject by asking questions.

For example:

Tanuki: えいごは むずかしい ですか。
Eigo wa muzukashii desuka.

Kitsune: いいえ、やさしい です。でも、つまらない ですよ。
Iie, yasashii desu, demo tsumaranai desu yo.

りか
すうがく
にほんご
おんがく
えいご
れきし
ちり
たいいく

すきな かもくは ________ です。

3 Tanuki secretly writes out his ideal timetable of six periods based on his favourite subjects. Kitsune finds out Tanuki's timetable by asking Tanuki's opinions about various subjects. When Kitsune gets a favourable opinion he must guess what period it is and fill in the timetable. *For example:*

abcde

Kitsune: りかは おもしろい ですか。
Rika wa omoshiroi desuka.

Tanuki: いいえ、つまらない です。
Iie, tsumaranai desu.

Kitsune: たいいくは たのしい ですか。
Taiiku wa tanoshii desuka.

Tanuki: はい、たのしい です。
Hai, tanoshii desu.

Kitsune: たいいくは 1じかんめ ですか。
Taiiku wa ichi-jikan-me desuka.

Tanuki: いいえ、2じかんめ です。
Iie, ni-jikan-me desu.

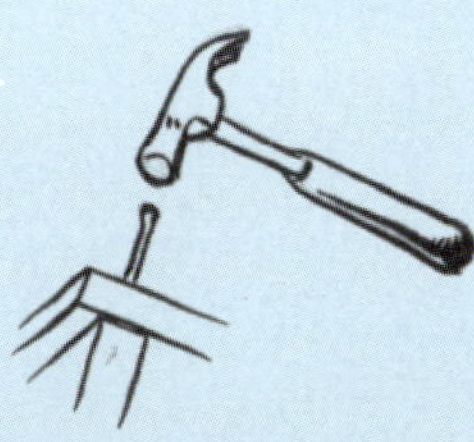

あいうえお

じかんわり Jikanwari Timetable	
1	
2	
3	
4	
5	
6	

4 Choose the most suitable expression from the list for each picture and put the number in the space provided.

1 にほんごは　おもしろい　です。

2 すずき　せんせいは　おもしろい　です。

3 たいいくは　たのしい　です。

4 たなか　せんせいは　きびしい　です。

5 せいこさんは　しんせつ　です。

にほんごわ

5 Karen is telling Masashi about her teachers. Draw a line from the teacher's name to Karen's comments.

Mr Yamada
kind
Mr Jones
entertaining
Ms Logan
so-so
Ms Smith
boring
Mr Parry
gentle
Ms Kelly
strict

6 Tanuki secretly writes down the name of a teacher whom you both know. Kitsune finds out who it is by asking questions. Tanuki answers only はい or いいえ. *Example:*

Kitsune: せんせいは　きびしい　ですか。
Sensei wa kibishii desuka.

Tanuki: はい。
Hai.

Kitsune: 30 さい　ですか。
Sanjuu-sai desuka.

Tanuki: いいえ。
Iie.

Kitsune: にほん　じん　ですか。
Nihon-jin desuka.

Tanuki: はい。
Hai.

Kitsune: たなか　せんせい　ですね。
Tanaka-sensei desu ne.

わかった！ Wakatta! I'VE GOT IT!

Asking if a subject is easy, difficult and so on	[Subject]	は	[adjective]	ですか。				
Agreeing that it is	はい、	[same adjective]	です。					
Disagreeing	いいえ、	[different adjective]	です。					
Asserting an opinion	[Subject]	は	[adjective]	です	よ。			
Making contrasting comments	[Subject]	は	[adjective]	です。	でも、	[different adjective]	です。	

あそびましょう！ Asobimashō!

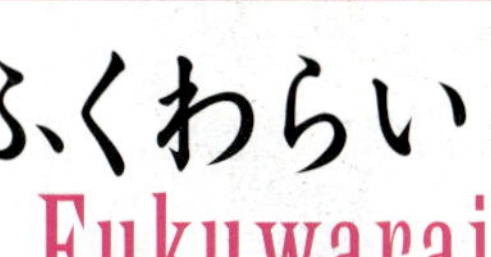

ふくわらい Fukuwarai

Fukuwarai is a game usually played at New Year. (*Fuku* means good fortune and *warai* means laugh.) A blindfolded person has to place the features onto a blank face board. Sets can be found in the shops in Japan, but you can easily make your own set with cardboard. You can use famous people's features to make it even more fun!

1. Draw a blank face on cardboard and cut out.

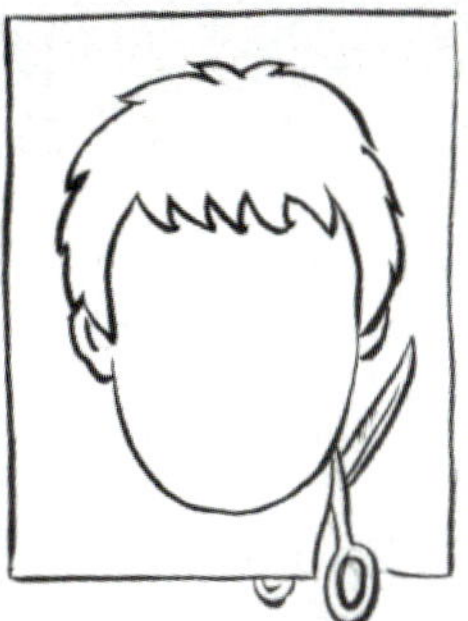

2. Make features.

3. In groups of 3–4, take turns to play.

インフォ
Info
DID YOU KNOW?

Club activities

Few Japanese students leave the school at the end of classes. Most remain there for several hours attending a club. Clubs are not compulsory, but most students join one or two. It is at the clubs that they meet people with similar interests and make friends. Choices are different from school to school, but these are some of the most popular.

第21回宇治市こどもまつり

Sporting	Cultural
Basketball	Art
Volleyball	Science
Baseball	English
Tennis	Drama
Soccer	Broadcasting
Judō	Concert band
Kendō	Choir
Archery	Ikebana

Sports clubs are said to be more demanding than cultural clubs because players are expected to practise in the morning before school, after school and at weekends. There are many interschool tournaments and games, and each school naturally wants its players to give their best performance.

Cultural clubs have their own productions, concerts, exhibitions and so on. Although they usually lack the competitive element, a lot of time and effort is put into these cultural activities.

Academic performance is also very important so clubs do not usually meet in the two weeks before exams. Students in the third year of kōkō, are usually too busy with study to belong to a club.

QUIZ

What do you know about school clubs?

Mark the following statements as true (T) or false (F). If you mark any false, give a reason.

1. All students belong to at least one club. ☐
2. Sports clubs practise before school. ☐
3. English is a cultural club. ☐
4. There is a wide variety of clubs to choose from. ☐
5. Students join clubs to make friends. ☐
6. Sports clubs are more demanding than cultural clubs. ☐

In most schools, Japanese students eat lunch inside their classrooms, sitting at their desks. To eat outside, standing or walking around, has always been considered bad manners in Japan. Although nowadays young people eat snack food on the street, schools insist on students sitting down inside to eat. You might be wondering about the leftovers from lunch. Well, Japanese students clean their own classrooms—and no one wants to make the job harder!

In *shōgakkō*, children eat *kyuushoku* (lunch provided by the school) with their teacher in the classroom. Each class has a roster of lunch monitors who bring lunch for the whole class from the school kitchens. The lunch menu is selected to provide the best nutrition and is expertly cooked. The food monitors wear aprons, masks and caps for hygiene.

In *chuugakkō* and *kōkō*, students bring lunch from home or buy something. Most schools have a canteen or tuckshop where students can buy sandwiches and snacks. Some schools have a dining area where students can order hot food like *tenpura soba* (deep fried, battered prawns and vegetables served with noodles in soup); *kareeraisu* (curry and rice); *tonkatsu ranchi* (a set menu of pork schnitzel, salad and rice) and so on.

Food that is brought from home is called *obentō* (packed lunch). It contains a variety of food which can include cooked and seasoned rice, omelette, fried chicken, vegetables and salad, pickles and some fruit. It is attractively packed in a special box which has segments for the different foods. The food chosen for *obentō* is food that will keep well, so sushi (raw fish on seasoned rice) is *not* included!

QUIZ

1 Which of the following foods would you *not* find in an obentō?

rice chicken soba tenpura
sushi soup fruit omelette
tonkatsu ranchi karee raisu vegetables

2 Which of the following students do *not* bring obentō to school?

a しょうがっこう 2ねんせい
b こうこう 3ねんせい
c ちゅうがく 3ねんせい

すきな たべもの

Sukina tabemono

ゆかりさんの すきな たべものは なん ですか。
Yukari-san no sukina tabemono wa nan desuka.

サンドイッチ
sandoitchi

てんぷら
tenpura

そば
soba

すし
sushi

ハンバーガー
hanbaagaa

ピザ
piza

ミートパイ
miitopai

やきとり
yakitori

ラザーニヤ
razaanya

ホットドッグ
hottodoggu

ケンくんの すきな たべものは なん ですか。
Ken-kun no sukina tabemono wa nan desuka.

Describing food

からい!
Karai!
あまい!
Amai!
おいしい!
Oishii!
まずい!
Mazui!

せつめい コーナー
Setsumei koonaa

Explanation corner

How do I ask what someone thinks?

The simplest way is to just say their name followed by は？ **wa.** For example: ゆかりさんは？ **Yukari-san wa?** This means *How about you Yukari?* or *What do you think, Yukari?*

We don't use the word for *you* very often; we prefer to use the person's name.

What should I say when I offer something?

To offer something, just say どうぞ **Dōzo.** This is a *very* useful expression! You can use it for inviting someone to sit down, to come this way, to offer food or drink—almost anything. It is similar to *Please*.

The answer to どうぞ **Dōzo** is ありがとう **Arigatō.** If you are thanking someone senior to you, you should say ありがとう ございます **Arigatō gozaimasu.**

Supposing I don't like certain foods?

It is rude to say that the food is まずい **mazui.** To express politely that you don't like it, all you have to say is: [The name of the food] は ちょっと … **wa chotto …**

This means literally, *It's a bit* … and leaves the rest to the imagination!

By the way, you can ask what Ken's favourite food is by saying, すきな たべものは なん ですか。**Sukina tabemono wa nan desuka.** or ケンくんの すきな たべものは なん ですか。**Ken-kun no sukina tabemono wa nan desuka.** This means both *What is your favourite food, Ken?* and *What is Ken's favourite food?*

To say My *favourite food*, you add の **no** to わたし or ぼく. わたしの すきな たべものは **Watashi no sukina tabemono wa** or ぼくの すきな たべものは **Boku no sukina tabemono wa.**

Particles

ぼくの すきな かもく
Boku no sukina kamoku

The little word の **no** is another particle. It signifies possession. Attached to わたし or ぼく, it changes *I* into *my*. Attached to any other noun, it works the same way as *'s* does in English. For example:

Person
or
place
の
no
Thing
It's
mine

せんせいの	**sensei no**	the teacher's
がっこうの	**gakkō no**	the school's

Saying what your favourite subject is

Asking another's opinion

ぼくの すきな かもくは たいいく です。
Boku no sukina kamoku wa taiiku desu.
カレンさんは？
Karen-san wa?
おんがく です。
Ongaku desu.

Asking someone's favourite food

Answering

ニッキーさんの すきな たべものは なん ですか。
Nikkii-san no sukina tabemono wa nan desuka.
ラザーニヤ です。
Razaanya desu.

Offering something

Saying thank you

Refusing

おべんとう です。どうぞ。
Obentō desu. Dōzo.
ありがとう。
Arigatō.
いいえ、おべんとうは ちょっと ...
Iie, obentō wa chotto ...

AB pp. 39, 40

できますか
Dekimasuka
CAN YOU DO IT?

1 Listen to the conversation and label the food item with the name of the person who says it is their favourite.

1 ______ 2 ______ 3 ______ 4 ______

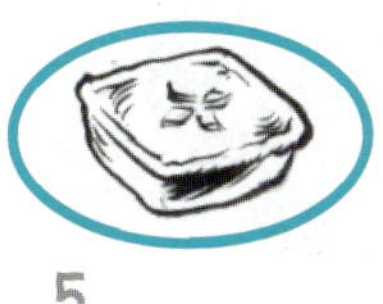   

5 ______ 6 ______ 7 ______ 8 ______

2 Akira works for a company that markets new snack foods. His job is to taste the food and make comments. Draw a line from each food item to his comment about it.

qwik pop
kapow
Pati
Frooty
Crispy
BIG pops

まずい mazui　からい karai　おいしい oishii　まあまあ maamaa　あまい amai

3 Kitsune chooses a favourite item from the menu and writes it down without showing Tanuki. Tanuki tries to guess the item by offering it. *For example:*

Tanuki: ピザ です。どうぞ。
Piza desu. Dōzo.

Kitsune: いいえ、ピザは ちょっと ...
Iie, piza wa chotto…

Tanuki keeps offering food until Kitsune says ありがとう Arigatō. Take turns.

メニュー
Menyuu
すし
sushi
ミートパイ
miitopai
サンドイッチ
sandoitchi
ハンバーガー
hanbaagaa
ピザ
piza
サラダ
sarada
やきとり
yakitori
てんぷら
tenpura
ホットドッグ
hottodoggu
そば
soba

けいようし ビンゴ

Keiyōshi bingo

おもしろい
たのしい
つまらない
まあまあ
むずかしい
やさしい
あまい
おいしい
からい
まずい
おもしろい
たのしい
つまらない
まあまあ
むずかしい
やさしい

Rules

Game 1

Play in threes. Kitsune must cross out all the adjectives on the diagonal cross. Tanuki must cross out the top line and the bottom line. The caller makes a list of all adjectives on the page and cuts the list into strips with one word on each strip. The caller randomly selects a strip and calls the adjective. The first person to cross out all their words calls out *Bingo*.

Game 2

Play in groups. Your teacher allocates a different line for each group and calls out the adjectives. The first group to cross out all their adjectives and say *Bingo* is the winning group.

わかった！ Wakatta! I'VE GOT IT!

Saying My *favourite* …	わたし ぼく	の	すきな	…				
Asking what someone's favourite ~ is	[Name]さん	の	すきな	~	は	なん	です	か。
Saying what someone's favourite ~ is	[Name]さん	の	すきな	~	は	~	です。	
Asking someone's opinion	[Name]さん	は？						
Offering (food and other things)	~	を	どうぞ。					
Accepting	ありがとう。	or	ありがとう　ございます。					
Declining	~	は	ちょっと。					

なに？　なに？ Nani? Nani?

What are they saying?

おべんとう

おべんとうは
おいしい　です。

すきな　たべものは
にほんの　たべもの
です。

ひらがな Hiragana

の	ろ	や	つ
no	ro	ya	tsu
の for not going north	ろ for a rose	や for yarn	つ for toothbrushing

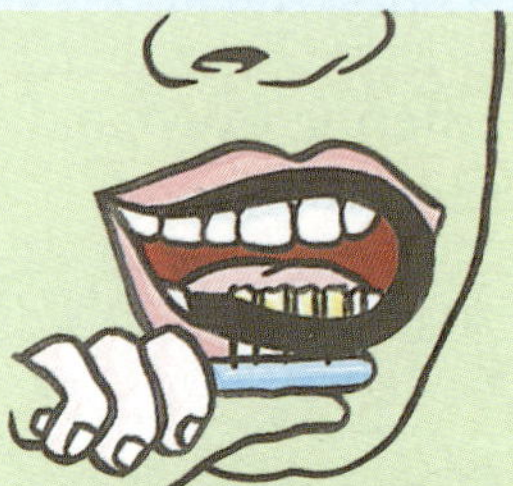

ら	あ	よ	む
ra	a	yo	mu
ら for run!	あ for acrobat	よ for a yacht	む for a mood

Remember to put a small っ before consonants you want to double.

For example, gakkō is written がっこう.

ん	わ	ら	や	ま	は	な	た	さ	か	あ
		り		み	ひ	に	ち	し	き	い
		る	ゆ	む	ふ	ぬ	つ	す	く	う
		れ		め	へ	ね	て	せ	け	え
	を	ろ	よ	も	ほ	の	と	そ	こ	お

AB pp. 43–46

ひらがな れんしゅう

Hiragana renshuu

1 Describe the food below by filling in the blanks. See the faces for hints.

a  か   い 

CHILLI
SAUCE

b  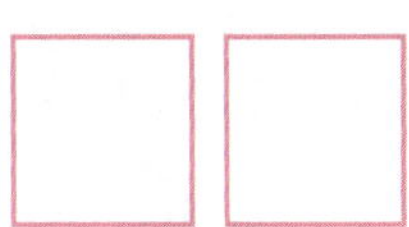 い 

Lollies

c  お  い 

d   い 

2 Describe the following subjects. See the faces for hints.

a おんがく  た  し

b えいご 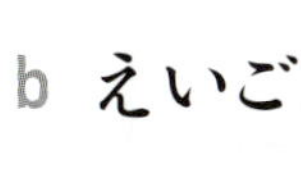  お も  い

c たいいく  ま  あ

d にほんご  さ し

3 Complete the conversation between Tanuki and Kitsune.

た　き___ねさん、りかは お___し___い ですか。

き　いいえ、___ま___ない です___。

た　すうがくは や___し___ですか。

き　いいえ、___ず___しい ですよ。

た　せんせいは しんせ___ですか。

き　はい。___さしい です。

てんせい

Lunchtime in the classroom ...

おべんとうは
まずい
ですね。
おべんとうは
おいしい　ですね。
SPORT

まずい　ですよ！

てんせいさん、
すきな　たべものは
なん　ですか。

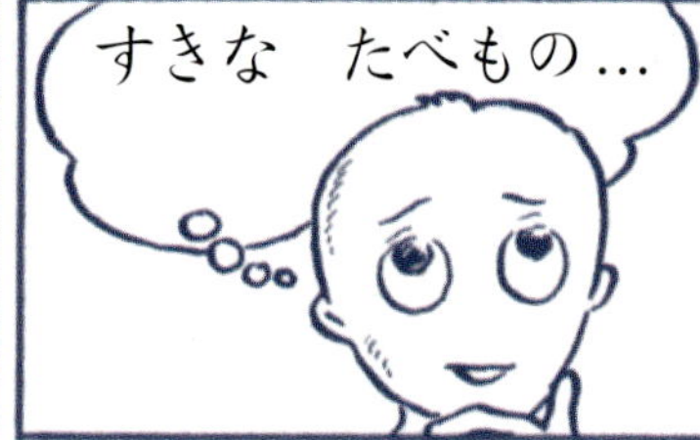
すきな　たべもの…

ばら　です！

ばら？
ばら？
ばら？
ばら？

ばらは
おいしい
ですよ。
SPORT

ばら！

AB pp. 47–48

チェック しましょう！
Chekku shimashō!

Let's check!

Describing subjects	
おもしろい	interesting
たのしい	fun
つまらない	boring
まあまあ	so-so
むずかしい	difficult
やさしい	easy

Expressions	
ありがとう	thank you (informal)
ありがとう ございます	thank you (formal)
ちょっと chotto	a bit
どうぞ dōzo	please, here you are
でも	but
そう ですね	that's right, isn't it

Pronouns	
ぼくの	my (boy talking, informal)
わたしの	my (girl talking, formal)

Food			
おべんとう obentõ	packed lunch	ハンバーガー hanbaagaa	hamburger
サンドイッチ sandoitchi	sandwiches	ピザ piza	pizza
すし	sushi	ホットドッグ hottodoggu	hot dog
そば soba	brown noodles	ミートパイ miitopai	meat pie
たべもの tabemono	food	やきとり yakitori	chicken on skewers
てんぷら tenpura	deep fried dish	ラザーニャ razaanya	lasagna

Describing teachers	
おもしろい	entertaining
きびしい kibishii	strict
しんせつ	kind
やさしい	gentle

Describing food	
あまい	sweet
おいしい	delicious
からい	spicy, salty
まずい	unpleasant tasting

I can:

- describe my subjects and my teachers
- ask for someone's opinion
- agree and disagree with someone's opinion
- offer food to someone
- say thank you or decline food politely
- describe food
- say what my favourite food is
- ask what someone's favourite food is
- read and write たのしい、おもしろい、むずかしい、やさしい、おいしい、あまい、からい、しんせつ

Unit 6

せんせい、みて ください

Sensei, mite kudasai!

Look at this, sensei!

1
Japanese class ...
みなさん、ふでと すみを
Mina-san, fude to sumi o
とって ください。
totte kudasai.
かみも とって ください。
Kami mo totte kudasai.
2
こくばんを みて ください。
Kokuban o mite kudasai.
日本
3
はい。みなさんも かいて ください。
Hai. Mina-san mo kaite kudasai.
日本
4
JAPAN
日本
5
ニッキーさん、
よく できました。
Nikkii-san, yoku dekimashita.
日本
6
むずかしい ...
Muzukashii ...

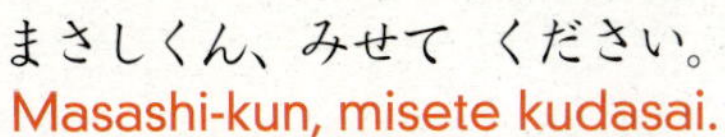
まさしくん、みせて ください。
Masashi-kun, misete kudasai.

7

8

もういちど かいて ください。
Mō ichido kaite kudasai.

はい。
Hai.

9

まさしくん、がんばって！
Masashi-kun, ganbatte!

10

せんせい、まどを しめても いい ですか。
Sensei, mado o shimetemo ii desuka.

はい。いい です。
Hai. Ii desu.

11

Ten minutes later …

あつい ですね。
Atsui desu ne.

あつい です。
Atsui desu.

12

あつい ですね。
Atsui desu ne.
ニッキーさん、
Nikkii-san
ドアを あけて
doa o akete
ください。
kudasai.

13

できました！せんせい、みて ください。
Dekimashita! Sensei, mite kudasai!

14

15
!?!

できますか
Dekimasuka
CAN YOU DO IT?

Can you find out how to say …

- Please take some paper.
- brushes and ink.
- Well done!
- Write it once more.
- May I close the window?
- Open the door, please.

せつめい コーナー
Setsumei koonaa

Explanation corner

How do I ask someone to do something?

To ask someone to do something you need to know some *please do* verbs. The word ください **kudasai** is similar in meaning to *please*. It follows a request. It is also used to mean *give me*.

Are you wondering about the difference between どうぞ **dōzo** and ください **kudasai**? どうぞ is short for どうぞ [request] ください。 It is a bit like *Please, please do it!* When it is obvious what you want someone to do, you only need to say どうぞ。

How do I say *Please say it again?*

If you do not hear clearly what someone says, say: あのう、もういちど いって ください。**Anō, mō ichido itte kudasai.** This means *Um, please say it again*. If you say, あのう **Anō,** which means *Um* or *Excuse me*, your Japanese will sound really natural!

もういちど **Mō ichido** means *once more*. Your teacher will use this a lot. For example: もういちど かいて ください。**Mō ichido kaite kudasai.** This means *Please write it again*.

WHAT A USEFUL EXPRESSION!

ね

ne

Isn't it?

ね is a special particle. It usually comes at the end of a sentence. It invites the listener to agree with the speaker. For example, あつい ですね *Atsui desu ne* means *It is hot, isn't it?*

Particles

ドアを あけて ください
Doa o akete kudasai

Did you notice that there is a little word を **o** before the request? This is particle を. It follows the object of the request and also the object of any action verb. For example: ドアを あけて ください。 **Doa o akete kudasai.** *Please open the door.*

The door is the object that we will open, so ドア **doa** is followed by the particle を。

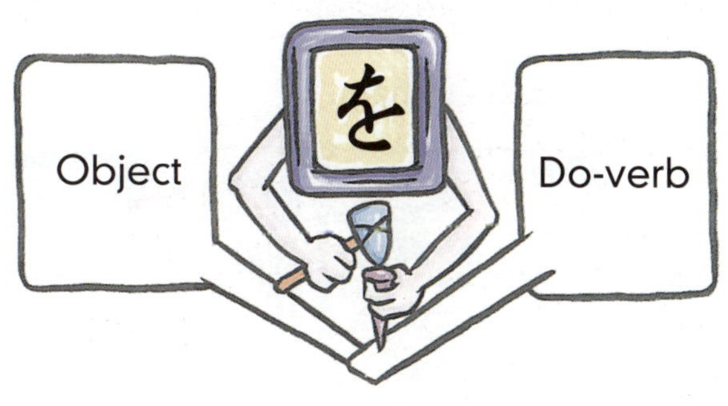
Object
を
Do-verb

Asking someone to take something

かみを とって ください。
Kami o totte kudasai.

Asking someone to show you something

ほんを みせて ください。
Hon o misete kudasai.

Asking someone to look at something

こくばんを みて ください。
Kokuban o mite kudasai.
あいう

Asking someone to close something

まどを しめて ください。
Mado o shimete kudasai.

Asking someone to open something

ドアを あけて ください。
Doa o akete kudasai.

Asking someone to do something again

もういちど かいて ください。
Mō ichido kaite kudasai.

AB p. 45

できますか Dekimasuka CAN YOU DO IT?

1 Listen to these conversations in a Japanese classroom. Label the pictures 1–8 in the order you hear them.

2 Kitsune points to any one of the pictures and says いって　ください Itte kudasai *(Please say it)*. Tanuki says the instruction that fits the picture.

Kitsune tries to trick Tanuki by pointing to another picture while saying もういちど　いって　ください Mō ichido itte kudasai *(Say it once more please)*. Tanuki must say the same thing or lose a point. Score a point for each correct response. Take turns.

日本
INK

3 Match the labels with the pictures. Write the number of the label in the space provided.

1 こくばんを　みて　ください。
2 みなさん、かいて　ください。
3 まどを　あけて　ください。
4 かみを　とって　ください。
5 ドアを　しめて　ください。

日本

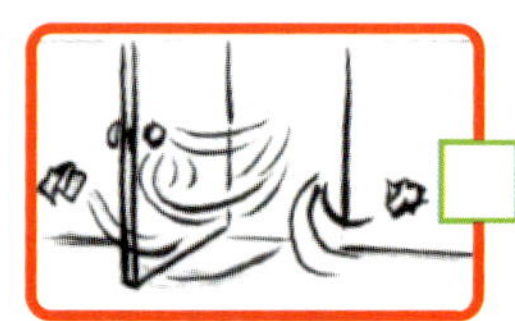

わかった！ Wakatta! I'VE GOT IT!

Asking someone to take something	[Object] を	とって	ください。
Asking someone to show you something		みせて	
Asking someone to look at something		みて	
Asking someone to close something		しめて	
Asking someone to open something		あけて	
Asking someone to write something		かいて	

Asking someone to say it again	(あのう、)	もういちど	いって	ください。
Asking someone to write it again			かいて	

べんきょう の こつ What's your secret?

Benkyō no kotsu

Karen, your pronunciation of Japanese is really good, and you seem to speak so fluently. I don't think Hiro always understands me when I try to speak to him. What did you do to become so good?
I listen to CDs, over and over again. Even when I was in the beginners' class. I listened as much as I could. I listen when I am doing chores around the house or when travelling in the car, on buses and trains. Other people think I am listening to music, but I am really studying Japanese. I find that it not only helps my pronunciation, it also helps me to remember the words and sentences. Of course in class I use Japanese as much as I can. Try it. You'll find it really works—and you'll enjoy it, I promise!

なに？ なに？

Nani? Nani?

What are they saying?

あのう、せんせい、
もういちど　いって
ください。

こくばんを
みて　ください。

さとうくん、
もういちど　みせて
ください。

AB p. 46

インフォ
Info
DID YOU KNOW?

More about Japan

Calligraphy

All Japanese children learn how to write with a brush. This is called *shodō* (calligraphy). Most school children have a *shodō* set for brush writing. A *shodō* set consists of special calligraphy brushes that are shaped so that they can write both thick and thin strokes; an ink stone that is rubbed on another stone to obtain the special *sumi* or calligraphy ink; a felt pad to place under the paper and weights to prevent the paper from moving.

Brush writing is taught to school children because it is considered to be a discipline of the mind and body and an important art form. To write well with a brush, the student must sit correctly, concentrate and breathe correctly. The brush must be held vertically. It takes many years of practice to master the art.

The belief that brush writing expresses the personality of the writer developed at the court of the Emperor of Japan in Heian times, more than 1000 years ago. Romances at the Heian court were conducted by writing poetry to each other. Ladies and gentlemen of the court would not only judge the character of the writer by the sensitivity of the poetry but especially by the skill of the calligraphy.

We know about this from one of the first novels ever written, the *Tale of Genji*, which was written with a brush in hiragana on 52 beautifully illustrated scrolls. The writer, Murasaki Shikibu, was a lady in the Heian court. In the *Tale of Genji*, which has been translated into English by Arthur Waley, the writer tells of the many romances of Prince Genji. The importance of beautiful brush writing features in every romance. The scrolls still exist and are kept in the National Museum in Kyoto.

Today, calligraphy contests are held regularly in Japan and calligraphy masters gain high prices for examples of their brush writing.

More about Japan

日本
にほん

Nihon

The Japanese people call their country *Nihon* or *Nippon*. Thousands of years ago, the Chinese called the islands to their east *Riben* 日本. The meaning of the characters they used are the *sun* and *origin* or *source*. They chose these characters because the source of the rising sun seemed to be the islands of Japan. The second character is also used for *book*. This is because a book can be thought of as the source of knowledge. Early travellers to China, heard the name *Riben* as Japan.

Shintō

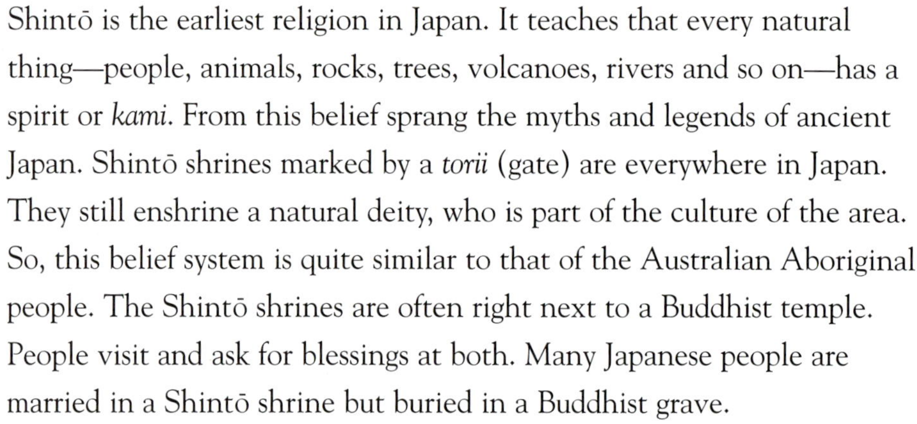

Shintō is the earliest religion in Japan. It teaches that every natural thing—people, animals, rocks, trees, volcanoes, rivers and so on—has a spirit or *kami*. From this belief sprang the myths and legends of ancient Japan. Shintō shrines marked by a *torii* (gate) are everywhere in Japan. They still enshrine a natural deity, who is part of the culture of the area. So, this belief system is quite similar to that of the Australian Aboriginal people. The Shintō shrines are often right next to a Buddhist temple. People visit and ask for blessings at both. Many Japanese people are married in a Shintō shrine but buried in a Buddhist grave.

別宮
風宮

Amaterasu the sun goddess

The characters for *Nihon* matched the legend that the sun goddess Amaterasu was the deity from whom the first emperor of Japan was descended. In the myths and legends of Japan, Amaterasu was created by one of the first two deities to appear, Izanagi and Izanami. They are said to have descended to earth from the heavens by a heavenly bridge—a rainbow. When they arrived, Izanagi stirred up the primeval ocean with his spear and the islands of *Nihon* were said to have formed from the droplets that fell back into the sea. The couple then created the rivers, mountains and all the features of the landscape. Finally Izanagi created the sun and the moon.

QUIZ

1 What do Japanese call Japan?
2 Why is it called Japan in the West?
3 Who was Amaterasu?
4 Can a person be a follower of both Buddhism and Shintoism?

いい ですか

Ii desuka

May I?

すわっても いい ですか。
Suwatte mo ii desuka.
ドアを あけても いい ですか。
Doa o akete mo ii desuka.
まどを しめても いい ですか。
Mado o shimete mo ii desuka.
かんじを かいても いいですか。
Kanji o kaite mo ii desuka.
ふでを とっても いい ですか。
Fude o totte mo ii desuka.
トムくんの ノートを みても いい ですか。
Tomu-kun no nooto o mite mo ii desuka.

どう いたしまして

Dō itashimashite

You're welcome

せんせい、すみません。
Sensei, sumimasen.
のりを かして ください。
Nori o kashite kudasai.
はい、どうぞ。
Hai, dōzo.
ありがとう ございます。
Arigatō gozaimasu.
どう いたしまして。
Dō itashimashite.

きょうしつで

Kyōshitsude

In the classroom

まど
mado
こくばん
kokuban
いす
isu
つくえ
tsukue
ちず
chizu
ドア
doa

In the drawer

のり
nori
ノート
nooto
えんぴつ
enpitsu
はさみ
hasami
けしゴム
keshigomu
いろえんぴつ
iroenpitsu

In the bag

じょうぎ
jōgi
ふでばこ
fudebako
ほん
hon
ぼうし
bōshi
かばん
kaban

せつめい コーナー
Setsumei koonaa

Explanation corner

How do I ask permission to do something?

This is really easy, just replace ください **kudasai** with ても いい ですか **temo ii desuka**. For example, すわって ください **suwatte kudasai** means *Sit down please.* すわっても いい ですか **Suwatte mo ii desuka** means *May I sit down?*

The answer is either, はい、いい です **Hai, ii desu,** which means *Yes you may* or いいえ、だめ です **Iie, dame desu,** which means *No, not now* or *No, you mustn't.*

How do I say *I've done it?*

When you have completed something you can say, できました **dekimashita.** This means *I have done it* or *I could do it.* It is related to できますか **dekimasuka,** which means *Can you do it?*

By the way, to praise someone you can say, よく できました **Yoku dekimashita.** This means *You have done it well.*

In Japan, we often say がんばって **ganbatte** to encourage someone. It is short for がんばって ください **ganbatte kudasai.** It means something like *Try hard* or *Don't give up.*

So, がんばってね。

I want to explain some more about saying *Thank you.* When you say ありがとう **arigatō** or ありがとう ございます **arigatō gozaimasu** to someone who has done something for you, they usually respond with どう いたしまして **dō itashimashite** or いいえ、どう いたしまして **Iie, dō itashimashite**. This means *You're welcome* or *No, it was nothing.*

いい ですか

Ii desuka

Asking permission

Granting permission

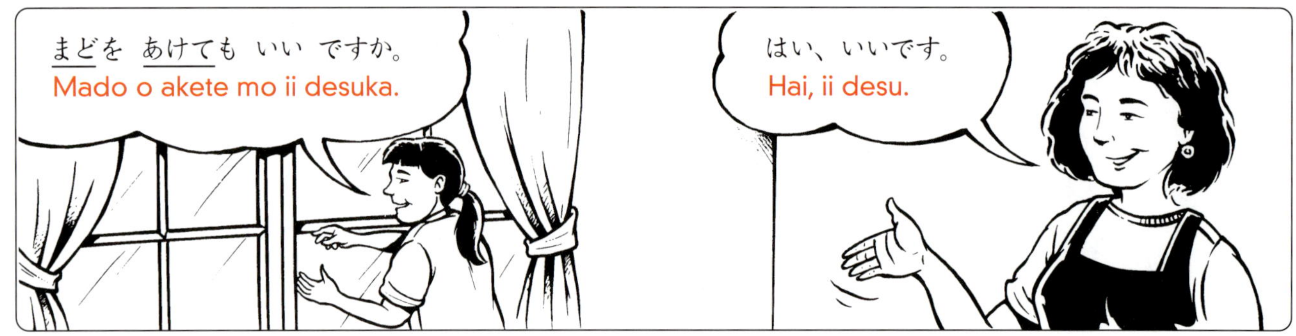
まどを あけても いい ですか。
Mado o akete mo ii desuka.
はい、いいです。
Hai, ii desu.

Refusing permission

みても いい ですか。
Mite mo ii desuka.
いいえ、だめです。
Iie, dame desu.

Giving praise

Offering encouragement

よく できました。
Yoku dekimashita.
がんばって。
Ganbatte.

Saying thank you

Responding (Don't mention it)

Saying I've done it

ありがとう(ございます)。
Arigatō (gozaimasu).
どう いたしまして。
Dō itashimashite.
できました。
Dekimashita.

AB pp. 47–48

できますか
Dekimasuka
CAN YOU DO IT?

1 Listen to the conversation between Masao and his teacher. What is Masao permitted to do? What is he not allowed to do.

2 You are helping Masako with her shopping for the school year. Write down what she says she needs in the order that you hear it.

3 Pretend that Kitsune has the powers to change into a person senior to Tanuki. Tanuki must ask to borrow all of the items in the picture below. *For example:*

Tanuki: はさみを かして ください。
Kitsune: はい、どうぞ。
Tanuki: ありがとう ございます。
Kitsune: どう いたしまして。

If Tanuki cannot remember the name of an item, Kitsune should encourage Tanuki by saying: がんばって and then saying the word. For example,がんばって たぬきさん。はさみ です。
When Tanuki completes a dialogue correctly, Kitsune must offer praise by saying, よく できました。

のり
ERASER

4 Take turns. Tanuki must try to reach the bowl of soba by asking Kitsune's permission at each obstacle. Kitsune can only refuse permission four times but tries to force Tanuki to the old bones. Every time permission is refused Tanuki must go a different way. If Tanuki cannot ask for permission accurately Kitsune is permitted an extra refusal. If Tanuki has to retrace his steps he has to ask again to pass the obstacle.

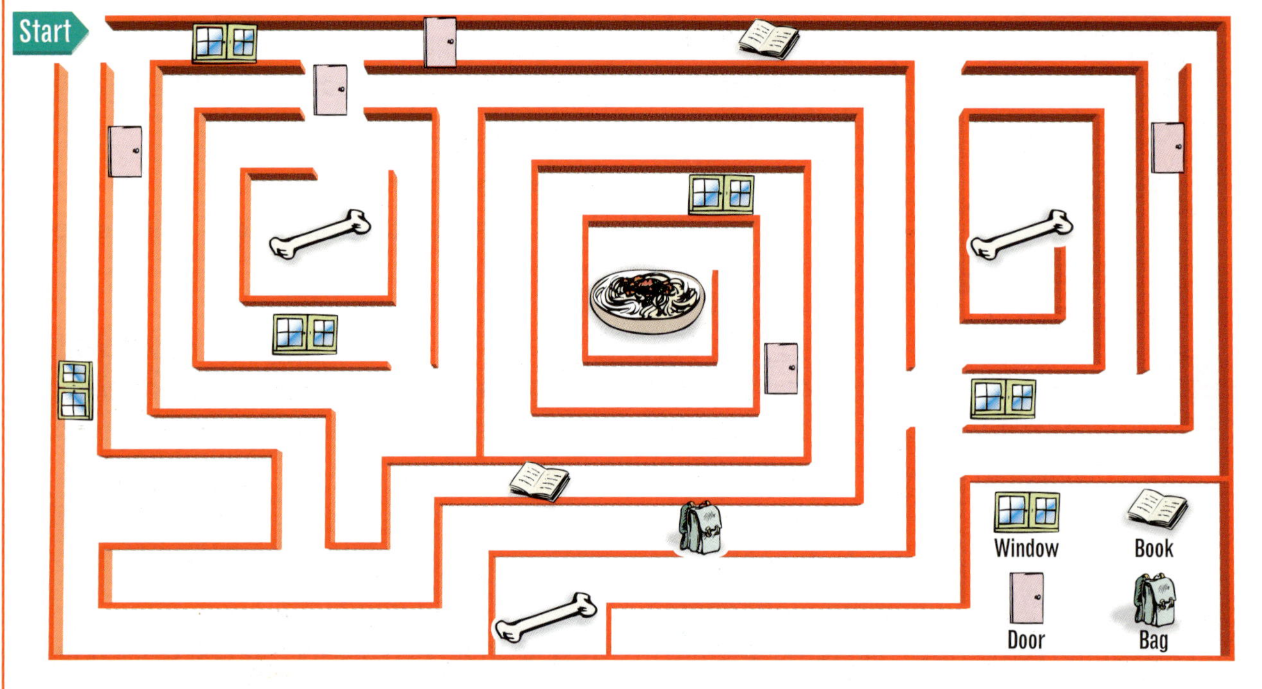

Start
Window
Book
Door
Bag

Example:

Tanuki: まどを　あけても　いい　ですか。
Kitsune: いいえ、だめ　です。
Tanuki: ドアを　あけても　いい　ですか。
Kitsune: はい、いい　です。
Tanuki: ほんを　よんで (あけて) も　いい　ですか
Kitsune: いいえ、だめです。
Tanuki: かばんを　あけても　いい　ですか。
Kitsune: はい、いい　です。

5 Choose the most suitable expressions for each picture. Place the appropriate letter in the speech bubble.

A+

a がんばって。
b せんせい、できました。
c ありがとう
d はい、どうぞ。
e よく　できました。
f どう　いたしまして。
g ありがとう
ございます。

ビンゴ

Bingo

いす	えんぴつ	いろえんぴつ	かみ
かばん	こくばん	じょうぎ	ちず
つくえ	のり	はさみ	ふで
ふでばこ	ほん	ぼうし	まど

Rules

Game 1

Play in threes. Kitsune must cross out all the nouns (*meishi*) on the diagonal cross. Tanuki must cross out the top line and the bottom line. The caller makes a list of all the nouns on the page and cuts the list into strips with one word on each strip. The caller randomly selects a strip and calls out the words. The first person to cross out all their words calls out *Bingo*.

Game 2

Play in groups. Your teacher allocates a different line for each group and calls the nouns. The first group to cross out all their nouns and say *Bingo* is the winning group.

わかった！
Wakatta!
I'VE GOT IT!

Asking permission	[Verb] ても	いい	です	か。
Granting permission	はい、	いい	です。	
Refusing permission	いいえ、	だめ	です。	
Responding to thanks	(いいえ、)	どう	いたしまして。	
Giving praise	よく	できました。		
Saying I have done it		できました。		

うたいましょう！ Utaimashō!

Let's sing! して ください の うた

みなさん こくばんを みてくだ さい (はい、せんせい！)
みなさん たってくだ さい
しずかに すわってくだ さい
ほんを よんでくだ さい

1 みなさん　こくばん　を　みて　ください　(はい、せんせい！)
みなさん　たっ　て　ください
しずかに　すわっ　て　ください
ほんを　よんで　ください

2 けんくん、えんぴつ　を　とって　ください　(ありがとう！)
ひらがなを　かいて　ください
ちょっと　みせて　ください
もういちど　かいて　ください

ひらがな Hiragana

み	け	を	す
mi	ke (げ ge)	o	su (ず zu)
み for mittens	け for kennel	を for orange	す for snail

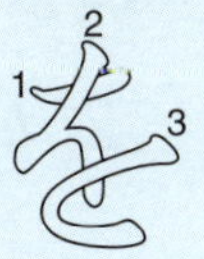

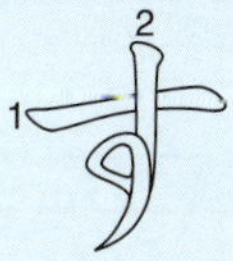

た	ち	ふ	ひ
ta (だ da)	chi	fu (ぶ bu)	hi (ぴ pi)
た for tap	ち for cheek	ふ for full	ひ for hippo

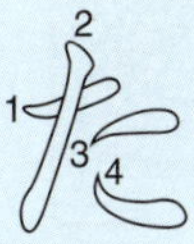

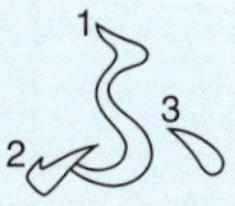

Remember the particle *o* is written を!

ん わ ら や ま は な た さ か あ
り み ひ に ち し き い
る ゆ む ふ ぬ つ す く う
れ め へ ね て せ け え
を ろ よ も ほ の と そ こ お

ひらがな れんしゅう

AB pp. 49–51

Hiragana renshuu

Hiragana exercises

1 Name the classroom items by filling in the blanks.

1 え＿＿＿

2 か＿

3 ＿＿

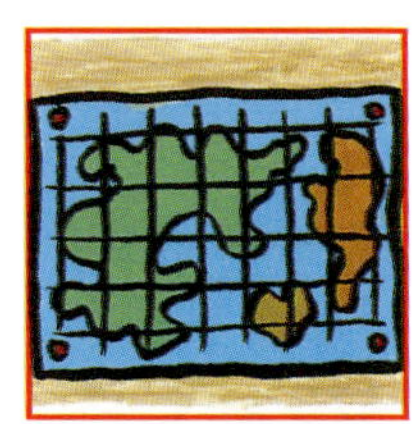

4 ＿＿ん

5 ほ＿

6 ＿さ＿

7 い＿

8 じょう＿

9 ＿で＿こ

2 Referring to the pictures, complete the sentences to make requests.

 1 かばんを ＿せて くだ＿＿。

 2 こくばん ＿＿て＿ださ＿。

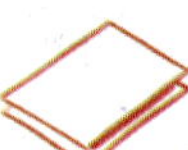 3 かみを ＿って く＿＿＿。

 4 ＿ど を ＿めて ＿＿＿＿。

 5 ＿＿を あ＿て ＿＿＿＿＿。

  6 ＿わって ＿＿さい。

 7 ＿って く＿＿い。

てんせい

かいて
ください。

yawn

えんぴつ？

てんせいくん、
えんぴつを
かして
ください。

えんぴつ…
えんぴつ…

??

えんぴつ！

はい、えんぴつ
どうぞ！

ど、どうも
ありがとう…

どう　いたしまして！

かみと　のりを
ください。

かみと
のり…

はい、
かみと　のり！

はさみも
かして
ください。

はさみ…

はい、はさみ、どうぞ！

AB pp. 52–53

チェック しましょう！ Chekku shimashō!

Let's check!

Classroom items	
いす	chair
いろえんぴつ	coloured pencil
えんぴつ	pencil
かみ	paper
かばん	bag
けしごむ	eraser
こくばん	blackboard
じょうぎ jōgi	ruler
すみ	calligraphy ink
ちず	map
つくえ	desk
ドア doa	door
ノート nooto	notebook
のり	glue
はさみ	scissors
ふで	brush
ふでばこ	pencil case
ほん	book
ぼうし	hat
まど	window

Expressions	
あのう…	Um, excuse me …
がんばって！	Try hard!
しずかに	quietly
できました	I've done it
どう いたしまして	You are welcome
もう いちど	once more
よく できました	Well done
はい、いいです	Yes, that's fine
いいえ、だめ です	No, not now

Adjective	
あつい	hot

Verbs for requests and asking permission			
あけて	open	いって	say
かいて	write	かして	lend
きいて	listen	しめて	close
すわって	sit	たって	stand
とって	take	みせて	show
みて	look	よんで	read
＋ください		Please …	
＋もいいですか		May I …?	

I can:

- understand eleven requests
- ask someone to do eleven things
- ask permission to do eleven things
- say that it is hot
- encourage someone
- respond to thanks
- ask someone to say it again
- say the names of most items in the classroom
- read and write こくばん、えんぴつ、ちず、みて ください、ほんを あけて ください、たって、すわって、みせて、かして、かいて、きいて ください、まどを あけても いい ですか。

part 3

Supootsu to rejaa

スポーツとレジャー

Sport and leisure

At the end of Part 3 you will be able to:

- ask and tell the time
- ask and say what time you do things
- ask and say where you are going
- ask and say who is going with you
- issue invitations
- ask and say what you did yesterday
- talk about transport.

Unit
7

しあいは　8じに　はじまります

Shiai wa hachi-ji ni hajimarimasu

The match starts at eight o'clock

1

2

せんせい　おはよう　ございます。

7じです。

おはよう。ケンくん、
Ken
いま　なんじ　ですか。

じゃ、ジョギングを
jogingu
はじめます。

3

せんせい、たいてい
なんじに　おきますか。

5じに　おきます。そして
トレーニングを　します。
toreeningu

うわあ、はやい。

4

せんせい、なんじに
ねますか。

9じに　ねます。

9じ？　はやい　ですね。わたしは
11じはんに　ねます。

5

11じはん！おそい　ですね。

6

みなさん、きいて　ください。あした、しあいは　8じに
はじまります。きょうは　9じに　ねて　ください。

でも、きょうは
パーティー　です。
paatii

7
パーティー？
Paatii?
じょうだん ですよ。
8
いま なんじ ですか。
7じはん です。
9
ひろくんは おそい ですね。
でんわ します。
10
11
もしもし。ひろくん ですか。
はい、わあ、せんせい？
12
あのう、なんじ ですか。
7じはん？すみません。
13
まって ください！

できますか
Dekimasuka
CAN YOU DO IT?

Can you find the expressions meaning …

- What time is it now?
- It's seven o'clock.
- Please wait.
- Wow, that's early!
- Please go to bed at nine today.
- The contest starts at eight.

せつめい コーナー
Setsumei koonaa

Explanation corner

How do I ask the time?

Shingo and I had to learn the words *time* and *o'clock*, to say *What time is it?* and answer *Two o'clock*.

In Japanese it's easier. Use the word じ **ji** for both. You can say あのう、なんじですか **Anō, nan-ji desuka** and answer 2じ です **Ni-ji desu**.

Careful! Four o'clock is よじ **yo-ji** and nine o'clock is くじ **ku-ji**.

Half past the hour is easy too: just say the hour and add はん **han**.

The word for minute is ふん **fun** but the pronunciation changes to ぷん **pun** after some numbers.

The changes are regular.

5, 15, 25, 35, 45 and 55 minutes are all ふん.

10, 20, 30, 40 and 50 minutes are all ぷん.

Can you guess why? See page 124.

To ask at what time someone does something say, なんじに… **Nan-ji ni …**

To answer, just say the time plus に **ni**, as in, 10じに **Juu-ji ni …**

WHAT A USEFUL EXPRESSION!

ちょっと まって ください

Chotto matte kudasai

This means *Please wait a minute.*

Particles

なんじに おきますか
Nan-ji ni okimasuka

The little word に looks the same as the に you learned which meant *in a place*, but it has a different meaning. This に always follows the time when you say that you do something at a certain time. When you just say the time you do not need に .

に
Action
Time

Asking the time

Saying the time

あのう、いま なんじですか。
でんわ
NEW YORK
7じ です。
LONDON
12じ です。
BERLIN
1じはん です。
BOMBAY
5じはん です。
TŌKYŌ
9じ です。
SYDNEY
10じ です。

Asking what time you go to bed and get up

Saying what time you go to bed and get up

なんじに ねますか。なんじに おきますか。
11じはんに ねます。そして、6じに おきます。
7じに ねます。3じに おきます。

いま、なんじ ですか
Ima nan-ji desuka

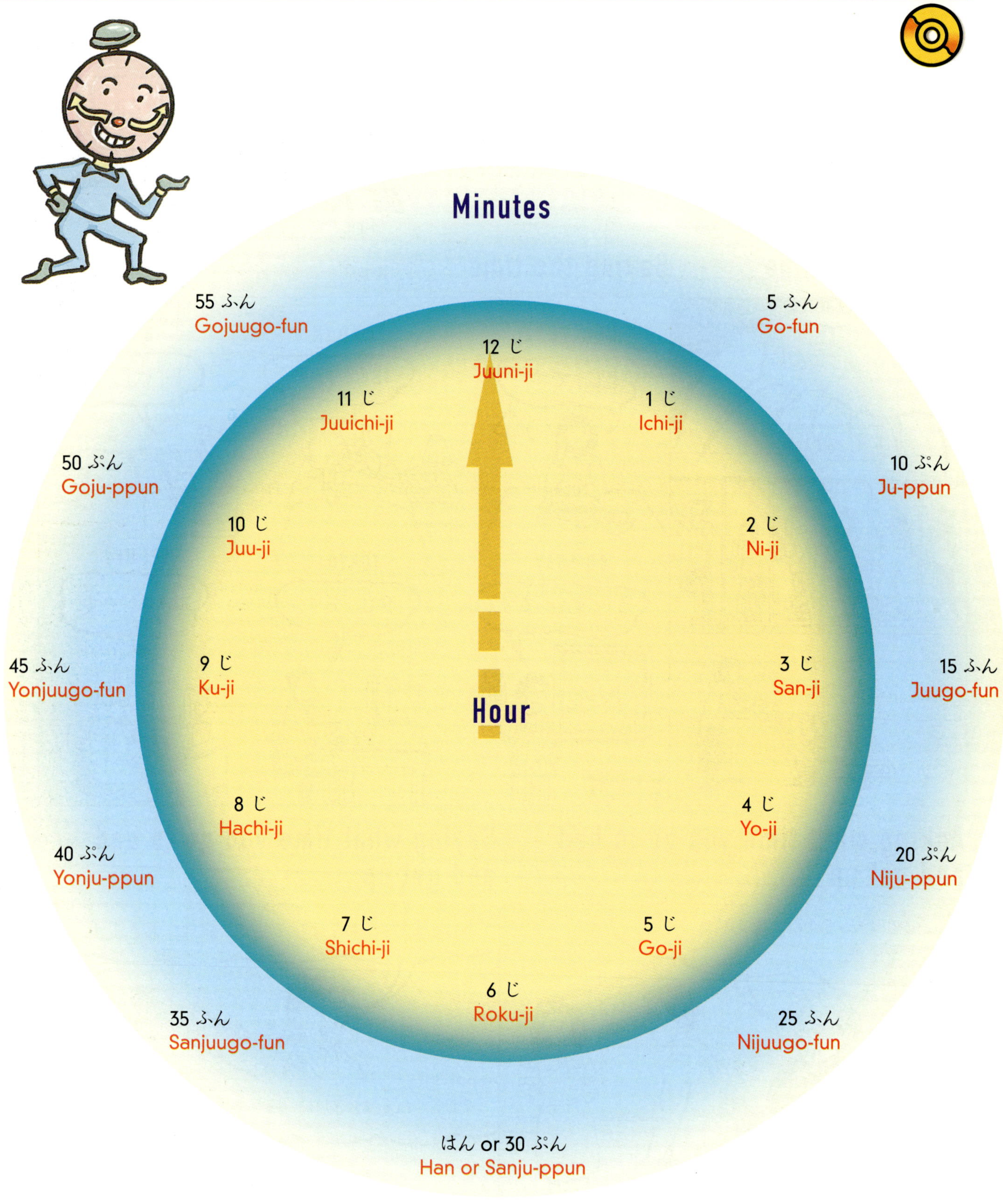
Minutes
12 じ
Juuni-ji
1 じ
Ichi-ji
2 じ
Ni-ji
3 じ
San-ji
4 じ
Yo-ji
5 じ
Go-ji
6 じ
Roku-ji
7 じ
Shichi-ji
8 じ
Hachi-ji
9 じ
Ku-ji
10 じ
Juu-ji
11 じ
Juuichi-ji
Hour
5 ふん
Go-fun
10 ぷん
Ju-ppun
15 ふん
Juugo-fun
20 ぷん
Niju-ppun
25 ふん
Nijuugo-fun
はん or 30 ぷん
Han or Sanju-ppun
35 ふん
Sanjuugo-fun
40 ぷん
Yonju-ppun
45 ふん
Yonjuugo-fun
50 ぷん
Goju-ppun
55 ふん
Gojuugo-fun

AB p. 59

できますか Dekimasuka
CAN YOU DO IT?

1 Listen to the times and mark whose watch is correct.

a
b
c
10:30
11:30
Tom
Johnny
Ken
Karen
Nicki
Naomi
Shin
Hiro
Tim

2 These people are at their bus stops. Listen to the times and mark which bus they can catch.

MORNINGS
5:45
6:40
6:59
7:40
8:00
8:45
9:05
9:40
10:11
10:45
11:40
MORNINGS
7:45
7:50
8:35
9:25
9:35
10:20
10:45
11:20
12:30
AFTERNOONS
12:11
12:45
1:40
2:11
2:45
3:40
4:11
4:45

3 Kitsune secretly writes down the time he or she gets up. Tanuki must find out what time Kitsune gets up by asking yes/no questions. *For example:*

Tanuki: 6じ 20ぷんに おきますか。
Roku-ji niju-ppun ni okimasuka.

Kitsune: はい or いいえ。

If the answer is いいえ Kitsune must add もっと はやい です Motto hayai desu (*It's earlier*) or もっと おそい です Motto osoi desu (*It's later*).

Take turns to be Tanuki and Kitsune. The second time around, use ねます nemasu.

ゲーム

You are Kitsune ninja and Tanuki ninja. You are trying to reach the treasure room in the ninja house. As you pass through the passages you must say the password: read aloud the time in Japanese. If you make a mistake you have to go back to the beginning. Kitsune times Tanuki's performance and vice versa. Who will get to the treasure house in the least time?

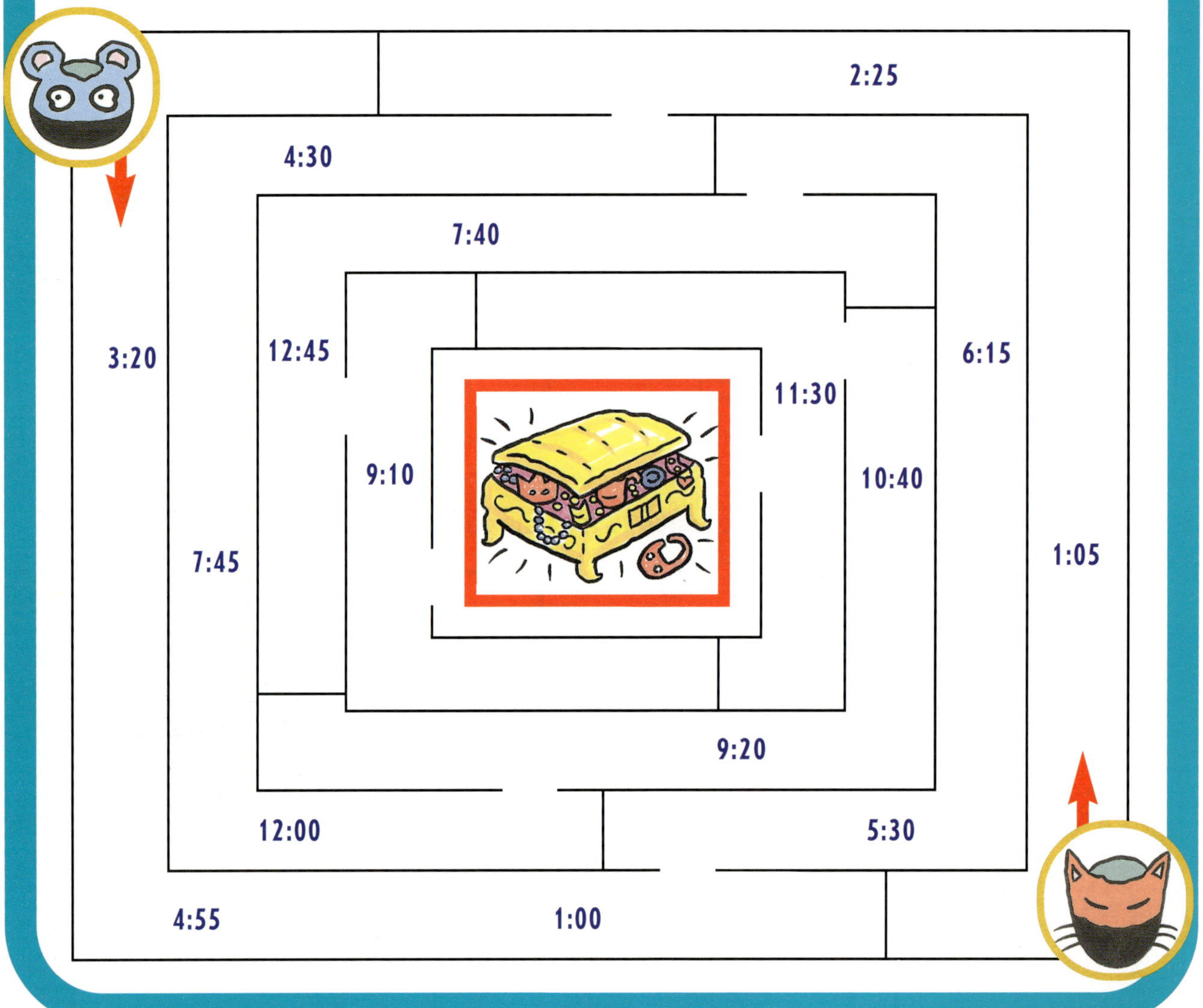

2:25

4:30

7:40

3:20 12:45 6:15

11:30

9:10 10:40

7:45 1:05

9:20

12:00 5:30

4:55 1:00

Hiragana puzzles

1 Complete the dialogues.

A: 6じ＿おきますか。

B: いいえ、7じ＿おきます。

A: あのう、＿＿なんじ　です＿。

B: 4じ＿＿です。

A: ＿＿じに　ねますか。

B: 8＿に＿ます。

A: はやい　です＿。

2 Match the sentences with their English meaning.

8じはんに　おきます。	8 o'clock is late.
8じに　ねます。	It is 8 o'clock.
8じ　です。	8 o'clock is early.
8じはん　です。	I go to bed at 8 o'clock.
8じは　はやい　です。	I get up at 8.30.
8じは　おそい　です。	It is 8.30.

わかった！ Wakatta! I'VE GOT IT!

To ask the time	あのう、	いま	なん	じ		ですか。
To give the time on the hour			1 … 12	じ		です。
On the half hour			1 … 12	じ	はん	です。
Hours and minutes	1 … 12 じ		5, 15, 25, 35, 45, 55		ふん	です。
	1 … 12 じ		10, 20, 30, 40, 50		ぷん	です。
Asking what time you get up/go to bed	なん	じ	に	おきますか。 ねますか。		
Saying what time you get up/go to bed	[Time]		に	おきます。 ねます。		

べんきょう の こつ What's your secret? Benkyō no kotsu

Are you writing a letter in Japanese, Ken?

Yes, it's to my Japanese penfriend, Michiko. We've been writing to each other since I was thirteen. I write in Japanese and she writes in English. That way we stay at the same level. In the beginning we couldn't say much, but we exchanged photos, maps of where we lived, stamps and used phone cards—that sort of thing. It really motivated me to learn to write better. She is always inviting me to go to stay with her family in Kyoto in the school holidays. I have been saving up for years and now I have enough to go!

AB p. 65

インフォ
Info
DID YOU KNOW?

The martial arts

Most Japanese martial arts were designed for self-defence. Later they developed into disciplines for the mind and body. Several of these martial arts have become popular in the West too. In Japan, traditional sports such as judō and kendō and even sumō are encouraged in high schools to instill self-discipline. Traditional sports are still very popular with everybody, though. Sumō, in particular, has a big following of devoted fans.

Sumō is considered to be the national sport of Japan. Fifteen-day tournaments are held six times a year across the whole nation. Even though the admission tickets are rather expensive, many people are happy to pay to watch the matches at the special venues; others follow them on TV.

Two wrestlers, called *rikishi*, have a wrestling bout on a ring called a *dohyō*. The wrestlers scatter salt to purify the *dohyō* before the match. This is an important ritual because it is considered that every match takes place in front of the gods and goddesses of Shintō. (See page 106.) The amount of salt thrown is more than 45 kilos a day!

There are seventy recognised winning throws and tricks. The loser is the wrestler who touches the *dohyō* with any part of his body other than the soles of his feet, or is pushed out of the *dohyō*.

The referee, called *gyōji*, is dressed in traditional costume and carries a fan-shaped object which is used to referee the game.

Each match is pretty short. Most take only around one minute, but it is very exciting when a smaller *rikishi* beats a larger opponent. When the audience become really excited, they often throw cushions and the like into the ring.

Sumō wrestlers' diets are highly specialised. The special food is called *chanko-nabe* (hot pot). It consists of a large amount of fish, meat and vegetables simmered together in a large pot.

High school sumō wrestlers

Judō is a combative technique that uses no weapons. Only throws and holds are allowed; hitting and kicking are not. Judō has been a regular Olympic event since 1964.

Karate is a form of unarmed combat using hands and feet. (Karate means empty hands.) It is said the sport came from Korea or Okinawa, the southern islands of Japan.

Kendō is Japanese fencing. Combatants use bamboo swords and body armour. They are only allowed to hit certain parts of their opponent's body.

Some Western sports are also very popular in Japan. Baseball, soccer, basketball, volleyball, gymnastics and athletics are especially popular and most schools have clubs for these sports. At universities, an even wider variety of clubs is available, such as American football, surfing, horse-riding, yachting, rowing, mountain climbing, rugby and so on.

However, some popular Australian sports are not well known in Japan, particularly netball and cricket. If you ever have a chance to play these sports with Japanese students, you will probably have to explain the rules to them.

まゆさんは　きょう　なにを　しますか
Mayu-san wa kyō nani o shimasuka

あさごはんを　たべます。
Asagohan o tabemasu.

ともだちと　テニスを　します。
Tomodachi to tenisu o shimasu.

ひるごはんを　たべます。
Hirugohan o tabemasu.

ゆかりさんと　べんきょう　します。
Yukari-san to benkyō shimasu.

ジョギングを　します。
Jogingu o shimasu.

ばんごはんを　たべます。
Bangohan o tabemasu.

ほんを　よみます。
Hon o yomimasu.

ひろくんは きょう なにを しますか Hiro-kun wa kyō nani o shimasuka

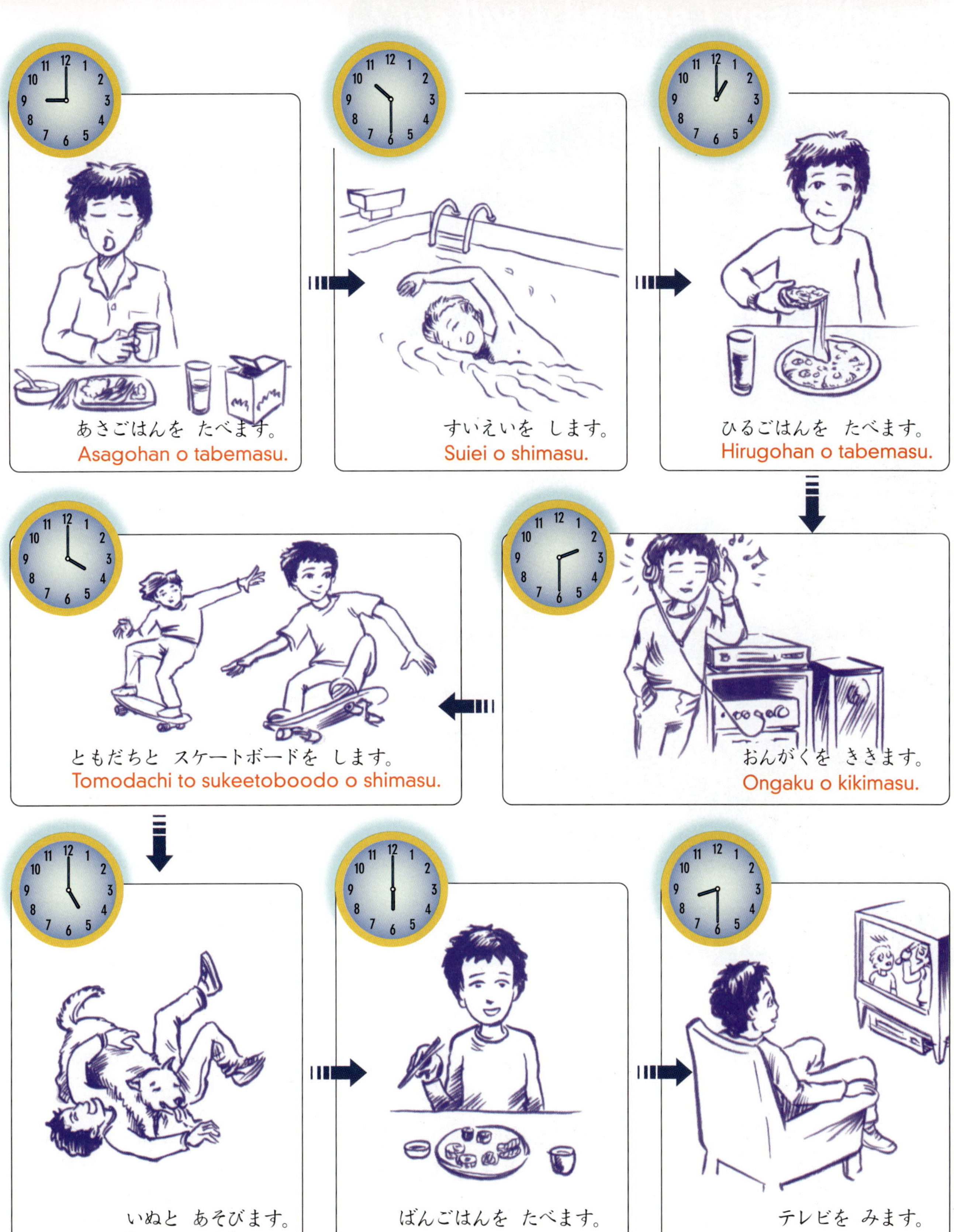

あさごはんを たべます。
Asagohan o tabemasu.
すいえいを します。
Suiei o shimasu.
ひるごはんを たべます。
Hirugohan o tabemasu.
おんがくを ききます。
Ongaku o kikimasu.
ともだちと スケートボードを します。
Tomodachi to sukeetoboodo o shimasu.
いぬと あそびます。
Inu to asobimasu.
ばんごはんを たべます。
Bangohan o tabemasu.
テレビを みます。
Terebi o mimasu.

せつめい コーナー
Explanation corner Setsumei koonaa

How do I say *I eat* and *I will eat*?

Yukari and I find English verbs very hard to learn. In English you say: I eat/we eat/you eat/you (all) eat/he, she or it eats/they eat.

In Japanese, we seldom use I, you, he, she, it, we and they. If it is unclear, we use a name. Also, there is no change to the end of the verb as you have in English. たべます **tabemasu** means *will eat* or *eat.* It just depends on the context.

Did you notice that all the verbs you have learned in this unit end with ます **masu**? This ending just shows that the speaker is speaking politely and that the action is in the present or future.

How do I say I eat *something*?

To say *I eat breakfast* the word for breakfast, あさごはん **asagohan**, is followed by the particle を **o**. This is the same を that you have already learned.

A lot of verbs are made up of a noun plus を します **o shimasu** which means *do.* For example, ジョギングを します **jogingu o shimasu.**

します also means *play*, as in *play tennis*: テニスを します **tenisu o shimasu.**

Particles

いぬと あそびます
Inu to asobimasu

The particle と to in the sentence いぬと あそびます Inu to asobimasu does not have the same meaning as the と you learned meaning *and*. This と means *accompanied by*, as in *with* a person or *with* an animal.

Person
or
Animal
と
to

Asking what time someone does something — Answering

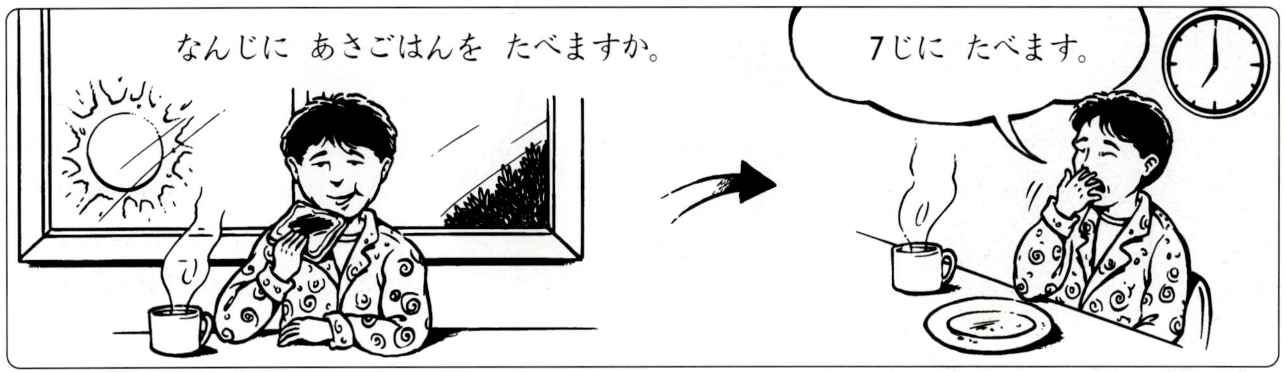
なんじに あさごはんを たべますか。
7じに たべます。

Asking if someone does something at a certain time — Answering

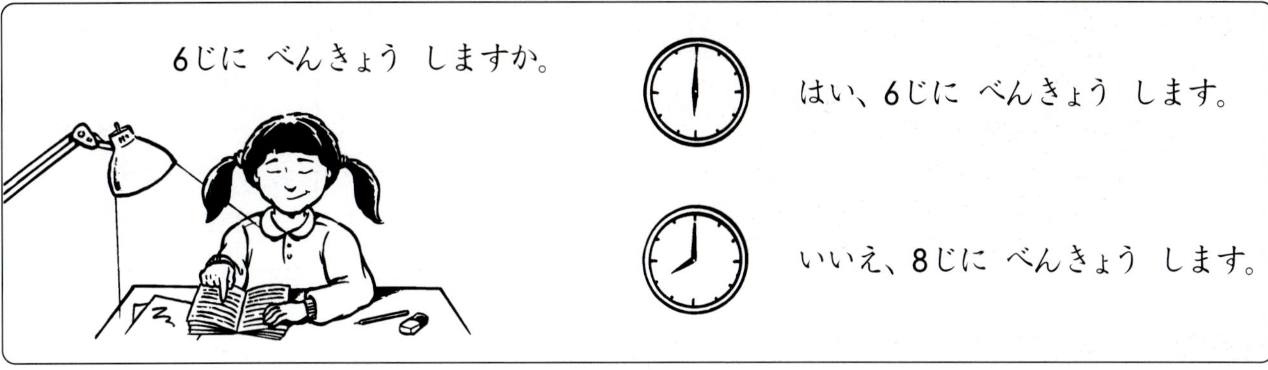
6じに べんきょう しますか。
はい、6じに べんきょう します。
いいえ、8じに べんきょう します。

Saying with whom you do things

いぬと あそびます。
ともだちと あそびます。

AB pp. 60, 61

できますか Dekimasuka

CAN YOU DO IT?

1 Tanuki chooses an identity from the pictures. Kitsune asks questions. Tanuki can only answer はい or いいえ until Kitsune guesses the identity.

For example:

Kitsune: 6じに たべますか。 Roku-ji ni tabemasuka. Tanuki: いいえ。

Kitsune: 6じに べんきょう しますか。 Roku-ji ni benkyō shimasuka. Tanuki: いいえ。

Kitsune: 4じに テレビを みますか。 Yo-ji ni terebi o mimasuka. Tanuki: はい。

Kitsune: けいこさん ですね。 Keiko-san desu-ne. Tanuki: はい。

Keiko
Eiji
Itsuko
Yōko
Saburō
Akira
Tsubasa
Emiko

2 The following friends of Akira believe they know his movements today. Listen to the passage and tick the statements that are true.

きょう、あきらくんは 6じに おきます。

きょう、あきらくんは 7じはんに あさごはんを たべます。

きょう、あきらくんは いぬと あそびます。
きょう、あきらくんは 9じはんに ねます。

きょう、あきらくんは 6じはんに テレビを みます。
terebi

3 Tanuki and Kitsune both secretly write down what time they will do the following today: eat breakfast, lunch and dinner, study, watch TV, go swimming and play with the dog. Remember: they always try to trick each other, so write down strange times!

Complete a profile on each other by asking questions.

For example: きつねさん、なんじに　あさごはんを　たべますか。

Hints	Kitsune's plans for today	Tanuki's plans for today
あさごはん	______	______
ひるごはん	______	______
ばんごはん	______	______
べんきょう	______	______
テレビ	______	______
すいえい	______	______
いぬ	______	______

4 Kitsune and Tanuki decide how they would like to spend the first day of their holiday. Secretly fill in the timetable of what you plan to do.

7.30
8.00
9.00
10.30
12.30
2.00
4.30
6.30

Copy a similar chart into your notebook. Fill it in after you have asked questions to find out each other's plans. *For example:*

Tanuki: きつねさん、8じに　なにを　しますか。
Kitsune: すいえいを　します。

Tanuki writes down '8 o'clock swimming'.

When you have finished, compare your timetable with your partner's. Are they the same? Here are some hints.

ばんごはんを　たべます。

テニスを　します。

すいえいを　します。

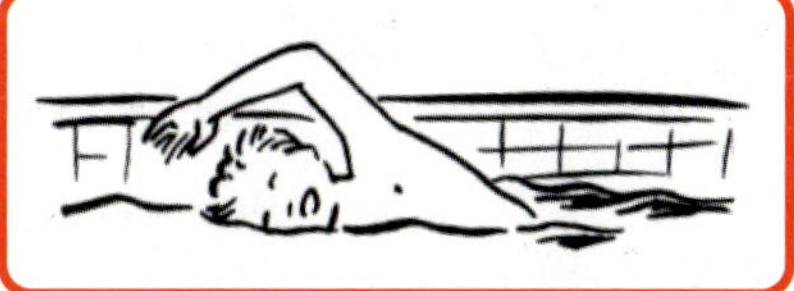

ともだちと　あそびます。

テレビを　みます。

ひるごはんを　たべます。

わかった！ Wakatta! I'VE GOT IT!

To ask what time you do something	なん	じ	に	[object] + を (optional)	しますか。	do
					たべますか。	eat
					ききますか。	listen
					よみますか。	read
					みますか。	watch
					べんきょう しますか。	study
				[no object]	あそびますか。	play, have fun

To ask if you do something at a certain time	[Time]	に	[object] + を (optional)	[verb] ますか。
To say what time you do things	[Time]	に		[verb] ます。
To say you do things with someone or with a pet	[Person/pet]	と		[verb] ます。

あそびましょう！ Asobimashō

Can you find any hiragana in the face? This face is called へのへのもへじ because it is drawn with these hiragana. Try drawing your own hiragana face. You can use other hiragana too, of course. Who can make the funniest face?

なに？ なに？

Nani? Nani?

What are they saying?

しあいは 10じに
はじまります。

がんばって！

11じに ともだちと スキーを します。
sukii
たのしい ですよ。

わたしたちは たいてい
4じはんに おきます。

12じに
ひるごはんを
たべます。

ひらがな

Hiragana

る	ひ	び	ふ	ぷ	へ	べ
ru	hi	bi	fu	pu	he	be

る for rude ruler

ひ for hippo

ふ for full

へ for helmet

ぬ	そ	ぞ	こ	ご	し	じ
nu	so	zo	ko	go	shi	ji

ぬ for nude

そ for saw

こ for cockatoo

し for shield

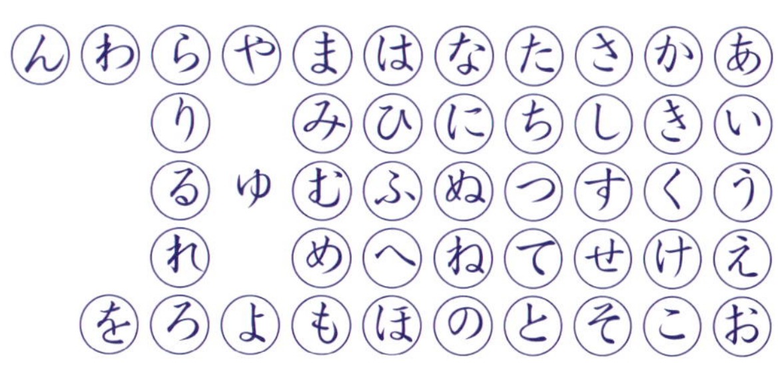

ん わ ら や ま は な た さ か あ
り み ひ に ち し き い
る ゆ む ふ ぬ つ す く う
れ め へ ね て せ け え
を ろ よ も ほ の と そ こ お

ひらがな れんしゅう

Hiragana renshuu

Hiragana exercises

1 Fill in the blanks to say what the people in the pictures are doing.

a 

あ 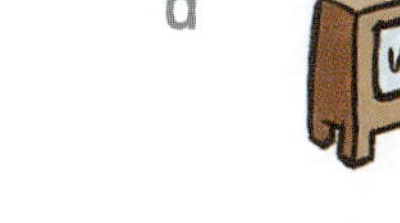 ます

b 

た □□ す

c 

き  ます

d

 す

e 

お 

f 

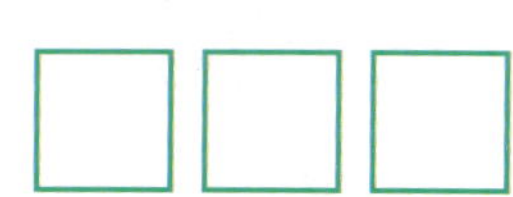

2 Complete both the questions *and* the answers!

a Q: ____ ____ じに あさ ____ ____ んを た____ ますか。
A: 7 ____ 25ふ ____ に たべます。

b Q: な ____ ____ に ____ ____ ごは ____ を たべますか。
A: 12じ 15 ____ んに たべます。

c Q: あのう、い ____ な ____ じ ですか。
A: 3じ ____ ん です。

d Q: あした なに ____ ____ ますか。
A: とも ____ ちと お ____ が ____ を ききます。
そして、い ____ と あ ____ びます。

e Q: おべん ____ うは おい ____ い ですか。
A: お ____ ____ い ですよ。どう ____ !

てんせい

てんせいくんは
なんじに　ねますか。

ぼくは...
12じに　ねます。

12じ？！
おそい　ですね！
?

CLICK

ばら！

ああ！おいしい！

BURP!
SPORT

てんせいくんは
きょう　なにを
しますか。

きょう...
ぼくは　いぬと
あそびます。
SPORTV

SPORTV

AB pp. 61–62

チェックしましょう！ Chekku shimashō!

Let's check!

Question words	
なんじ	What time?
なに	What?

Adjectives	
おそい	late
はやい	early

Expressions	
うわぁ	Wow!
そして	then
どうも	very much, really
たいてい	usually
もっとはやい	earlier
もっとおそい	later
あとで	after that

Time words	
あした	tomorrow
いま	now
きょう	today
じ	o'clock, hour
はん	half
ふん、ぷん	minute

Verbs	
あそびます	play, have fun
おきます	get up
ききます	listen
します	do, play
たべます	eat
ねます	go to bed
はじまります	begin
べんきょう します benkyō shimasu	study
みます	watch, look at

Requests	
おきて ください	Please get up
きて ください	Please come
ねて ください	Please go to bed
まって ください	Please wait

Nouns	
あさごはん	breakfast
いぬ	dog
ジョギング jogingu	jogging
しあい	match, game
じょうだん jōdan	joke
すいえい	swimming
スケートボード sukeetoboodo	skateboard
テニス tenisu	tennis
テレビ terebi	TV
ともだち	friend
トレーニング toreeningu	training
ひるごはん	lunch
ばんごはん	dinner

I can:

- ask for and say the time
- say what time I go to bed and get up
- ask others what time they go to bed and get up
- say what time I do six other things
- ask others what time they do six other things
- say that it is early and late
- understand four more requests
- describe three martial arts
- read and write what time my friends and I do things.

1
2
3
4
5
6
7
8
9

Unit 8

どこへ いきますか

Doko e ikimasuka

Where are you going?

1

GRAND FETE
Eaton Park
10.00am

2

あ、なおみさん！

3

こんにちは！
どこへ　いきますか。

こうえんへ
いきます。

4

ぼくも！
だれと　いきますか。

ジョニーくんと。
Jonii

5

あ、ジョニーくん。

こんにちは。

6

7

あ、たなか　せんせい！

8

せんせい、こんにちは。
どこへ　いきますか。

やあ、こうえんへ
いきます。
みんなは？

9
ぼくたちも　こうえんへ　いきます。いっしょに　いきましょう。
10
せんせい、いっしょに ひるごはんを　たべましょう。
11
ひるごはん？ えーっと、ひるごはんは ちょっと …
12
ぼくは　ホットドッグを hottodoggu たべます。
ひとみ さん♥
13
TON PARK
じゃあ、また。
14
ああ、せんせいは デート　です。 deeto
あ、せんせい。
15
ごめんなさい。
じゃあ、ぼくたちも。
え？みんな デート？ deeto ひどい！

できますか
Dekimasuka
CAN YOU DO IT?

Can you find the expressions meaning …

✱ Where are you going?
✱ Who are you going with?
✱ Let's go together.
✱ I'm going to the park.
✱ Let's eat lunch together.
✱ I'm going to eat hot dogs.
✱ What? Everyone on a date? Awful!

せつめい コーナー
Setsumei koonaa

Explanation corner

How do I say *Where are you going?*

大正橋·難波
Taishobashi Nanba
天王寺駅
Tennoji Sta.
天満橋
Tenmabashi

To ask where someone is going just say どこへ　いきますか。**Doko e ikimasuka.**

To answer that you are going to Tennōji say, てんのうじへ　いきます。**Tennōji e ikimasu.**

Notice that in the answer you replace the word どこ **doko**, which means *where*, with the place name.

By the way, many Japanese people say, どこに　いきますか。**Doko ni ikimasuka** instead of どこへ　いきますか。**Doko e ikimasuka.**

You can use either へ **e** or に **ni** in the question and the answer.

How do I say *Who are you going with?*

To find out who is going with someone say, だれと　いきますか。**Dare to ikimasuka.**

To answer that you are going with Ken say, **Ken** さんと　いきます。**Ken-san to ikimasu.**

Notice that you replace だれ **dare** (*who*) with the name of the person.

By the way, teachers may say みなさん **minasan** when speaking formally to students but use みんな **minna** in informal situations. Notice that it is spelt differently.

WHAT A USEFUL EXPRESSION!

ごめんなさい
Gomen nasai

This just means *sorry*!

Particles

どこへ いきますか
Doko e ikimasuka

The particle へ e indicates direction. It is similar in meaning to the English preposition *to* as in *to a place*. It follows どこ doko when asking where someone is going and follows the place named in the answer.

Notice that particle へ is written with hiragana へ he. The particle に ni can be used instead of へ.

Place
へ or に
Direction verb

Asking where someone is going **Saying where you are going**

どこへ いきますか。
(に)
おおさかへ いきます。
(に)
アメリカへ いきます。
Amerika (に)
がっこうへ いきます。
(に)
こうえんへ いきます。
(に)

Asking who is going with someone **Saying who is going with you**

だれと いきますか。
ひろくんと いきます。
だれと うみに いきますか。
なおみさんと
いきます。
?

できますか
Dekimasuka
CAN YOU DO IT?

1 Take turns. Kitsune secretly writes down a place from line 1, a person from line 2 and an activity from line 3. Tanuki must find out Kitsune's plans by asking questions. Kitsune only answers はい or いいえ. For example:

Tanuki:	おおさかへ　いきますか。	Kitsune:	いいえ。
Tanuki:	たなか　せんせいと　いきますか。	Kitsune:	はい。
Tanuki:	テニスを　しますか。 tenisu	Kitsune:	いいえ。

おおさか Oosaka	こうえん kōen	うみ umi	とうきょう Tōkyō	やま yama

Karen

Mr Tanaka

Ken

Johnny

Naomi

2 Listen to the passage and complete Naomi's schedule for today.

9:00	
10:30	
11:30	
12:30	
4:00	
6:30	

3 Follow the lines and say where each person is going.
どこへ　いきますか。

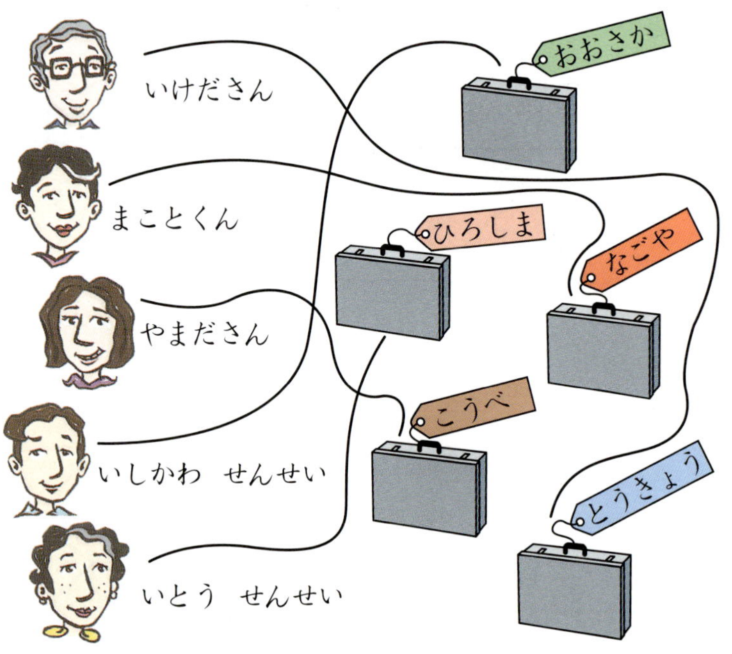
いけださん
まことくん
やまださん
いしかわ　せんせい
いとう　せんせい
おおさか
ひろしま
なごや
こうべ
とうきょう

どこへ いきますか、みなさん？ Doko e ikimasuka, minasan?

AB p. 65

Give each person a name and say where they are going.

For example: ケン (Ken) さんは うみに いきます。サーフィン (saafin) を します。

うみに いきます。サーフィンを Saafin します。

にほんへ いきます。

まちへ いきます。えいがを みます。

かわへ いきます。つりを します。

やまに いきます。キャンプを Kyanpu します。

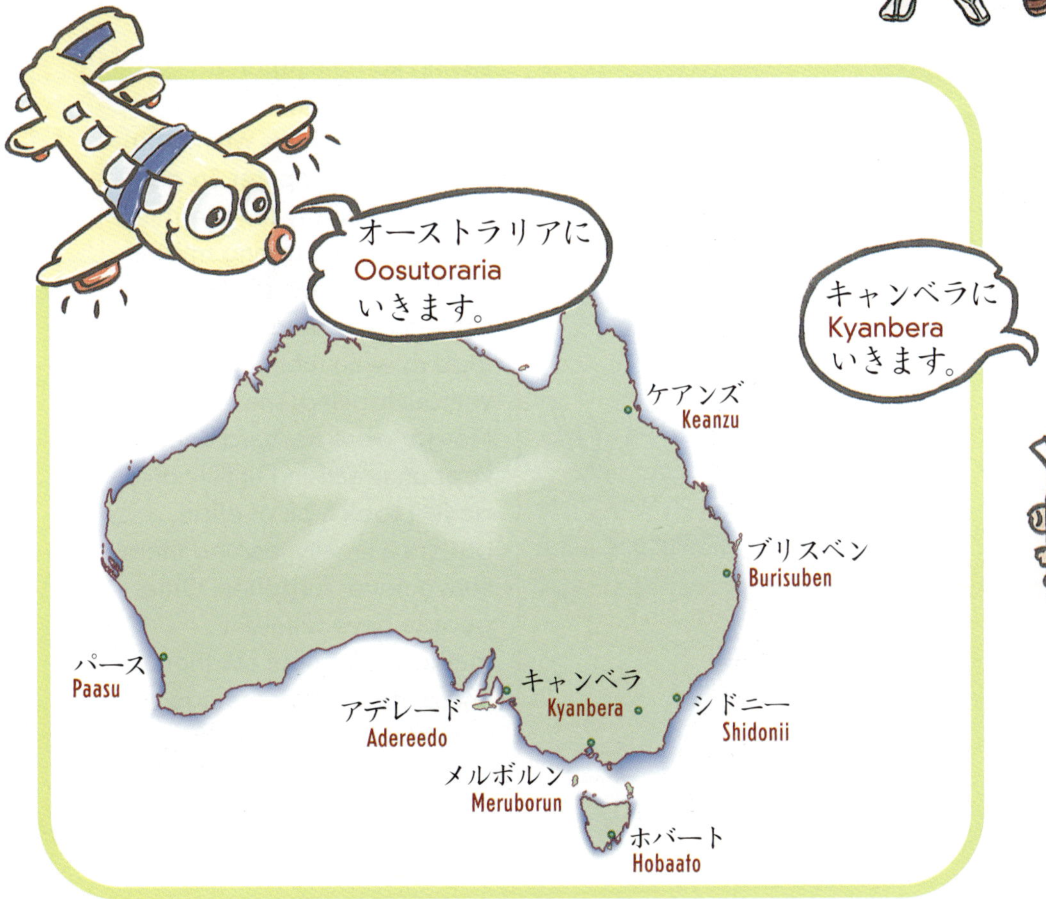

オーストラリアに Oosutoraria いきます。

キャンベラに Kyanbera いきます。

ケアンズ Keanzu
ブリスベン Burisuben
パース Paasu
アデレード Adereedo
キャンベラ Kyanbera
シドニー Shidonii
メルボルン Meruborun
ホバート Hobaato

わかった！ Wakatta! I'VE GOT IT!

Asking where someone is going	どこ	へ or に	いきますか。
Saying where you are going	[Place]	へ に	いきます。
Asking who is going with someone	だれ	と	いきますか。
Saying who is going with you	[Name]	と	いきます。

べんきょう の こつ Benkyō no kotsu

How did you learn hiragana, Karen? I try to remember them but I keep forgetting.
Well, it is to do with short-term and long-term memory. When you try to memorise something it goes into your short-term memory. Unless you make an effort to get it into your long-term memory it disappears. It is a bit like saving something on a computer. If you forget to save, it disappears when you turn off the computer. To get hiragana into my long-term memory I kept testing myself. I copied out new words and sentences in hiragana. I then tried to write them again without looking. The syllables I forgot were my hard ones. I kept on practising until I could do it. It took a bit of effort, but once I really learned them I have never forgotten. Other people have different methods. Why not ask them and decide which method suits you best?

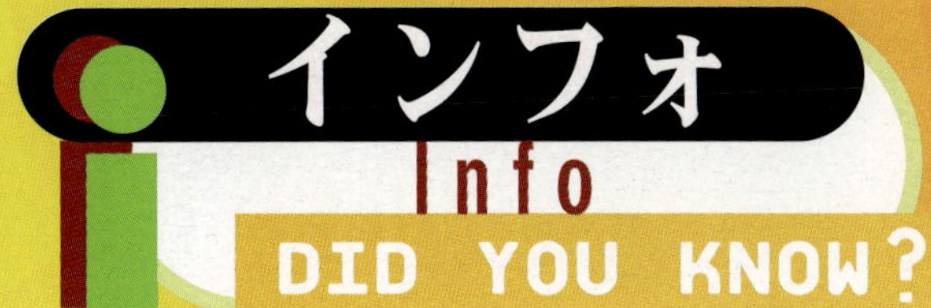
インフォ
Info
DID YOU KNOW?

The history of kanji

The first kanji characters were written by the descendants of people who inhabited the valley of the Yellow River in China more than 7000 years ago. Inscriptions found on thousands of oracle bones discovered in Xiaotun have been dated to more than 3000 years ago. Some of the characters are exactly the same today. From the others, scholars have traced how the characters changed over time.

The oracle bones were used when the king of Shang wished to contact the spirits of his ancestors to ask for advice. The diviners (readers of the messages from the spirits) inscribed the king's questions on the bones of oxen or the shells of turtles. They then bored rows of hollows into the bone and put a heated stick into the hollows. The bone cracked and in the cracks the diviners were able to read the answers.

Poor peasants had been digging up these ancient bones for centuries and selling them to apothecaries to make Chinese medicine. They were called dragon bones. No one noticed the inscriptions until 1903 because the peasants used to clean the bones to make them smoother. The inscriptions caused a sensation because of the amount of information they gave about life in the Shang dynasty, more than 3000 years ago.

How have they changed?

羊
魚
鳥
馬

Complex ideas

Of course, only simple concrete items can be represented by a picture. The ancient people of China developed thousands of characters to write down their language, and they combined parts of characters to convey more complex ideas.

For example, water is written 水. This is shortened to three drops of water and appears on the side of characters that have something to do with water.

For example:

the sea	海
a pond	池
the beach	浜
the ocean	洋

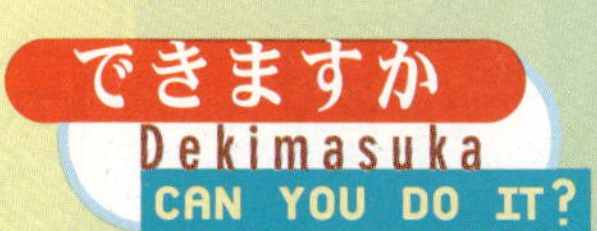
できますか
Dekimasuka
CAN YOU DO IT?

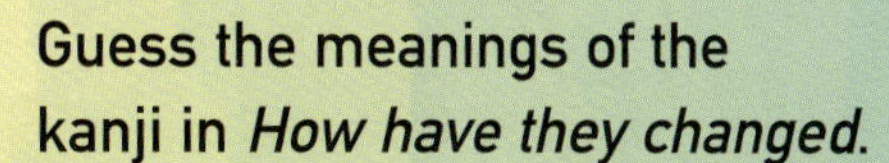

1 Guess the meanings of the kanji in *How have they changed*.

2 Find out about as many other languages as you can that are not written using the alphabet.

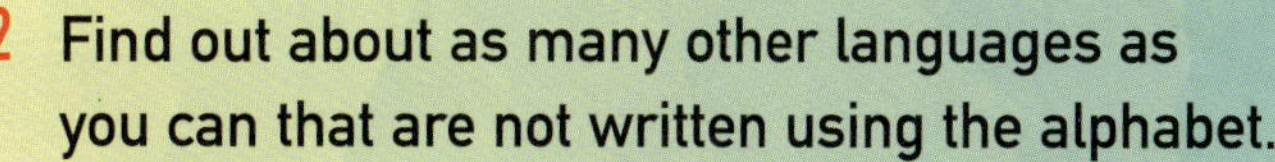

3 Make up your own picture writing and write a message.

ぶんかさい

Bunkasai

ぶんかさい
きょうは　ぶんかさい　です。
がっこうへ　いきましょう。
たのしい　ですよ。
えいがを
みましょう。
ええ、
みましょう。
おばけやしき
おばけやしきに
いきましょうか。
いいえ、おばけやしきは
ちょっと…
そう　しましょう。
やきとりを
たべましょうか。
おいしい　ですか。

ポップコーンを
poppukoon
たべましょう。
どうぞ！
ありがとう。
コーラスを
Koorasu
ききましょうか。
ききましょう。
いっしょに
ゲームを　しましょう。
geemu
はい、
しましょう。

せつめい コーナー Setsumei koonaa

Explanation corner

How do I say *Let's go*?

To say *Let's go* change the ます **masu** ending of いきます **ikimasu** to ましょう **mashō** and say, いきましょう **ikimashō**.

You can say いっしょに **isshoni** first to make it even clearer that it is an invitation. If I wanted to invite Yukari to my school's Open Day I would say いっしょに ぶんかさいに いきましょうか **Isshoni bunkasai ni ikimashō ka.**

If she accepted she would say, はい、いきましょう **Hai, ikimashō** or そう しましょう **Sō shimashō.**

If not she would say, ぶんかさいは ちょっと… **Bunkasai wa chotto …** or いまは ちょっと… **Ima wa chotto …**

By the way, you can change all the verbs you know into invitations by changing the ending to ましょう **mashō.** For example, たべましょう **tabemashō** means *Let's eat.*

You can also easily make a question: たべましょうか **Tabemashō ka** *Shall we eat?*

How do you make plurals?

We do not often use plurals in Japanese. For example, いぬ **inu** can be dog or dogs. Most of the time it is obvious what we mean.

Sometimes, though, we need to make it clearer. For example, if two people are telling a third what they are going to do, they need to say *we*. A common plural ending for people is たち **tachi.** A boy would say ぼくたち **boku-tachi** and a girl would say わたしたち **watashi-tachi.**

いっしょにいきましょう

Isshoni ikimashō

Asking someone to go with you | **Agreeing** | **Refusing**

いっしょに　こうえんへ
いきましょう。

はい、いきましょう。

こうえん→

ええっと、こうえんは
ちょっと …

Inviting someone to do something | **Agreeing** | **Refusing**

いっしょに　やきとりを
たべましょうか。

そう　しましょう。

はい、たべましょう。

ええっと、やきとりは
ちょっと …

いっしょに　マドンナを
Madonna
ききましょうか。

そう　しましょう。

はい、ききましょう。

ええっと、マドンナは
Madonna
ちょっと …

いっしょに　えいがを
みましょうか。

そう　しましょう。

はい、みましょう。

MOVIE

ええっと、えいがは
ちょっと …

いっしょに　ジョギングを
jogingu
しましょうか。

そう　しましょう。

ええっと、ジョギングは
jogingu
ちょっと …

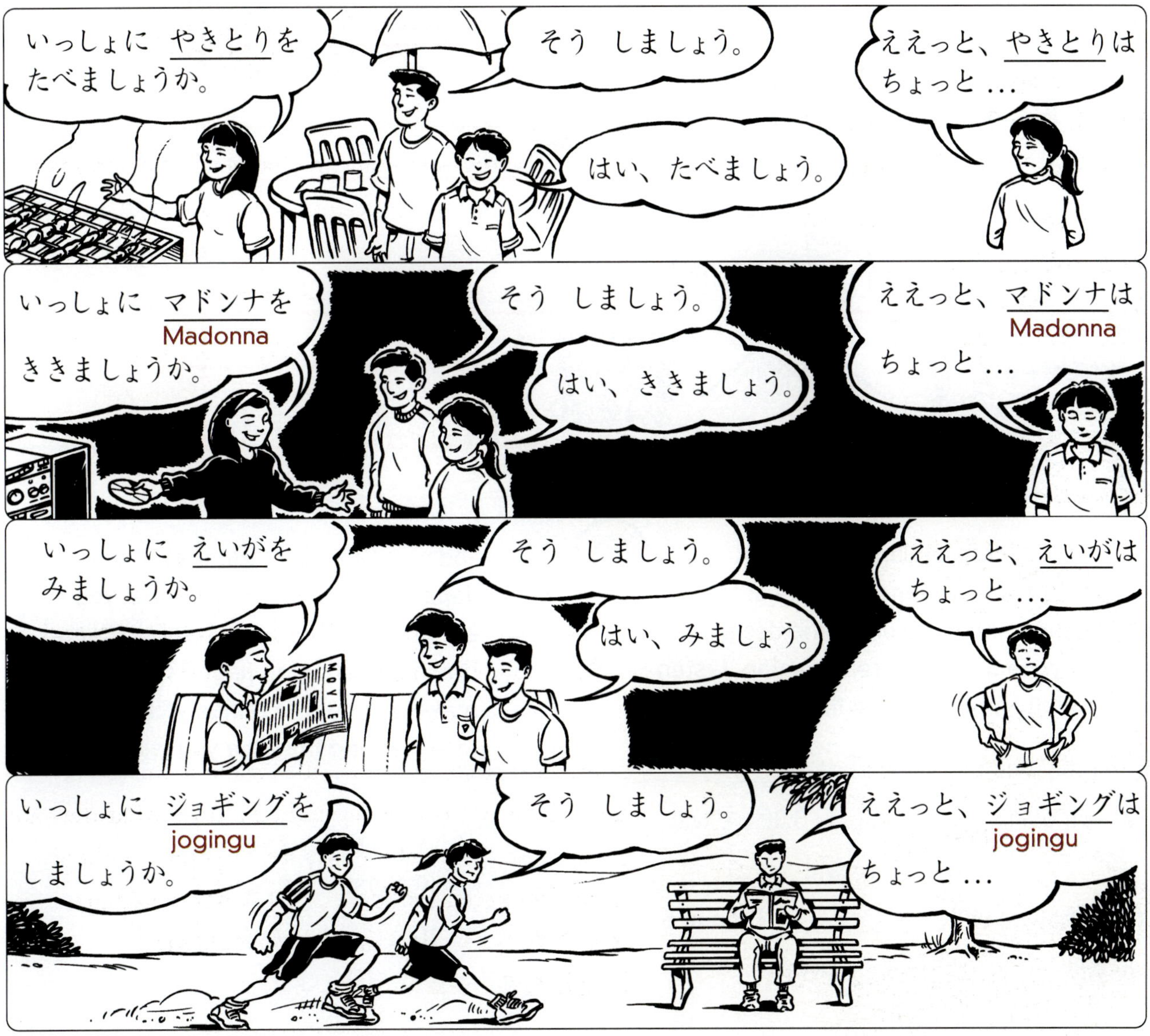

AB pp. 69

できますか Dekimasuka

CAN YOU DO IT?

1 Tanuki and Kitsune must come to an agreement on what they are going to do today. Copy the schedule below into your notebook.

Kitsune starts. Decide which activity to suggest from each group. Use 〜ましょうか to ask Tanuki's opinion. Tanuki agrees or refuses. If Tanuki refuses he or she offers another suggestion. Keep going until agreement is reached.

Now they must decide what time to do each activity. Tanuki asks なんじに〜ましょうか。 Kitsune suggests a time and Tanuki agrees or disagrees and suggests another time.

Continue until you agree and then complete the schedule.

1
______を します。
2
______を たべます。
3
MATHS
ENGLISH
JAPANESE
______を べんきょうします。
4
______に いきます。
Your schedule
9:00
11:00
1:00
3:00
5:00
7:00
9:00

2 The judo club is planning a party. You have to keep the minutes of the meeting and write down the decisions. Everyone has a different opinion. Listen carefully and complete the summary.

The judo club party will start at ____________.
We will eat ____________. At 3.30 we will ____________. At 4.00 we will ____________.
After that we will ____________. Then at 5.30 we will ____________.

3 Today is Open Day (Bunkasai) at a Japanese school. Imagine that you are going with Hiro or Naomi. Using the information on pages 150 and 151 make a list of the things you will do together and the time you will do them.

a きょうは なおみさんと ぶんかさいに いきます。

b 10じに えいがを みます。

ゲーム Game

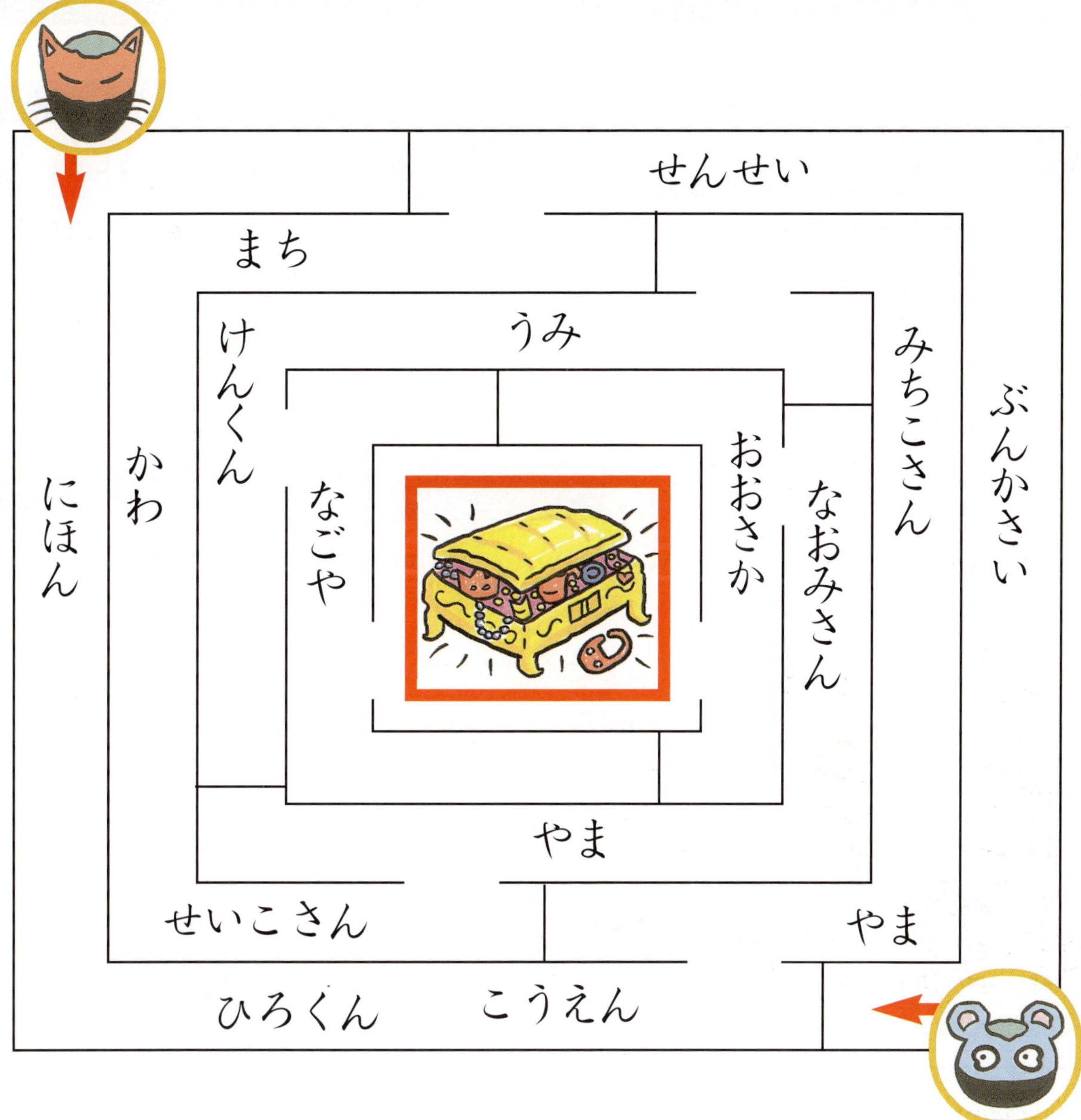

せんせい
まち
うみ
けんくん
みちこさん
ぶんかさい
かわ
にほん
なごや
おおさか
なおみさん
やま
せいこさん
やま
ひろくん
こうえん

You are Kitsune ninja and Tanuki ninja. You are trying to reach the treasure room in the ninja house. As you pass through the passages you must say the passwords. The password is any sentence that includes the word written in the passageway. For example, ぶんかさいに　いきましょう or ケンくんと　いきます. If you make a mistake you have to go back to the beginning. Take turns to say your own password. Listen very carefully to what your partner says, because you should be finding their mistakes! Who will get to the treasure house first?

わかった！ Wakatta! I'VE GOT IT!

	[Optional]	[Optional]	Verb
Inviting someone to go with you	いっしょに	[place] へ or に	いきましょう（か）。
Inviting someone to eat something	いっしょに	[food] を	たべましょう（か）。
Inviting someone to listen to something	いっしょに	[thing] を	ききましょう（か）。
Inviting someone to watch something	いっしょに	[thing] を	みましょう（か）。
Inviting someone to do something	いっしょに	[thing] を	しましょう（か）。
		[Optional]	Verb
Accepting an invitation	はい、	いっしょに	～ましょう。
	はい、		そうしましょう。

あそびましょう Asobimashō!

Setsubun is a festival held in early February, when winter turns to spring. Each town has a unique way of celebrating *setsubun*. The most common way is called *mamemaki*, which involves bean throwing. People scatter beans around to drive out demons and bring in good fortune. In some temples and shrines they have *oni* (demon) dances. You can make an *oni* mask with cardboard, rubber bands and some wool. Here's how.

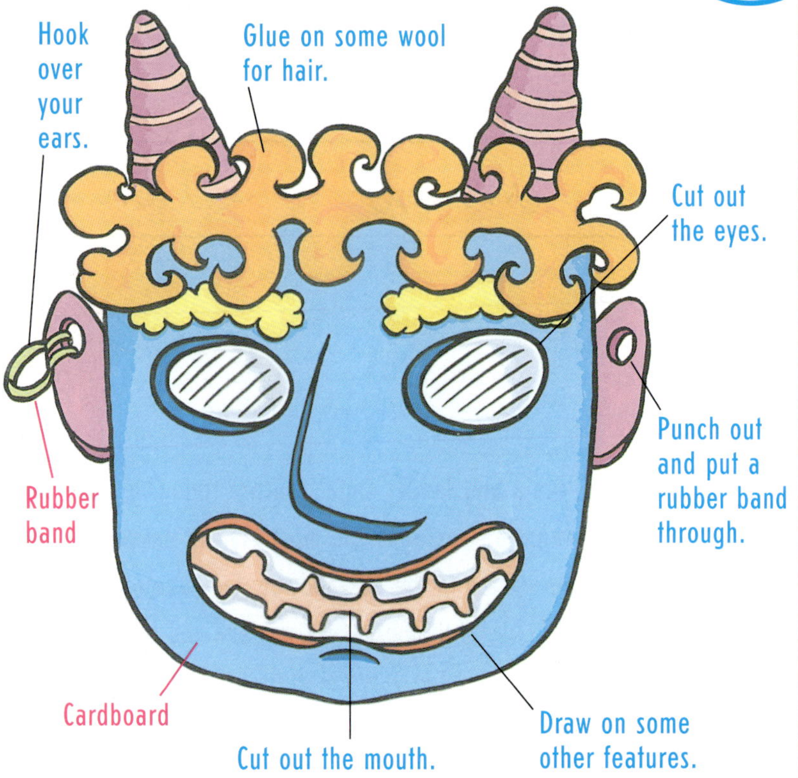

Hook over your ears.
Glue on some wool for hair.
Cut out the eyes.
Punch out and put a rubber band through.
Rubber band
Cardboard
Cut out the mouth.
Draw on some other features.

なに？なに？

Nani? Nani?

What are they saying?

いっしょに　まちへ
いきましょう。

開運福だるま
江戸久
鉄砲漬
うりの鉄砲漬
福よせ

いっしょに　かわへ
いきましょう。

いっしょに　こうえんへ
いきましょう。いぬと
あそびましょう。

30

いっしょに　てんぷらを
たべましょう。
おいしい　ですよ。

インフォ
Info
DID YOU KNOW?

えんそく
Ensoku

南町奉

If you visit Japan in April or September you will be surprised to find thousands of uniformed Japanese middle-school students visiting the same interesting places that you have chosen. Spring and autumn are the popular seasons for *ensoku* or school excursions and the whole year group is expected to attend. Special excursions for particular subjects are not encouraged because students would be missing classes.

Japan is a very old civilisation and there are thousands of castles, temples, shrines and museums to visit to gain an understanding of Japan's history. Students can gaze over the inland sea where the Minamoto, led by Yoritomo defeated the Taira in the 12th century. They can visit a castle where magnificently painted screens depict the battle scene. They can visit a museum where the armour worn by the samurai of the time is displayed. They can also visit tranquil tea houses set in beautiful gardens that were designed for feudal barons centuries ago.

Other school excursions are designed for students to gain an appreciation of the natural beauty of Japan and its ancient culture. Students are taken to the mountains, lakes or to quiet coastal areas to hike and camp. In these areas, the many legends associated with the landscape are often marked in some way. For example, Meoto Iwa are a pair of huge rocks. The larger is considered to be male and the smaller female. They are tied together with five sacred ropes, which are replaced three times a year by local young men. The rocks mark a holy place where legend says a god is enshrined in a sacred stone 700 metres from the shore, just under the water. Hearing the ancient stories, students gain a deeper appreciation and understanding of their culture and literature.

In the last year of junior and senior high school, a special school excursion called *shuugaku ryokō* is held. Some schools visit the capital city, Tōkyō, the ancient capital, Kyōto, or the Peace Park in Hiroshima, which was built on the site of the epicentre of the first atomic bomb used in warfare. Some schools take students overseas.

QUIZ

1 Find out more about the Taira, the Minamoto and Yoritomo. 2 Find out more about Japanese gardens.

ひらがな Hiragana

や	ゆ	よ
ya	yu	yo
 や for yarn	 ゆ for useful utensil	 よ for yacht

Example words:

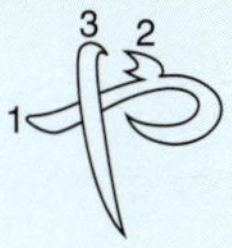		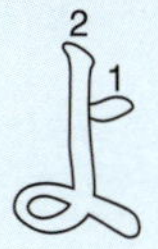	
きゃ kya	きゅ kyu	きょ kyo	きょう kyō べんきょう benkyō
しゃ sha	しゅ shu	しょ sho	いっしょに isshoni いきましょう ikimashō
ちゃ cha	ちゅ chu	ちょ cho	ちょっと chotto ちゅうがっこう chuugakkō

ん	わ	ら	や	ま	は	な	た	さ	か	あ
		り		み	ひ	に	ち	し	き	い
		る	ゆ	む	ふ	ぬ	つ	す	く	う
		れ		め	へ	ね	て	せ	け	え
	を	ろ	よ	も	ほ	の	と	そ	こ	お

ひらがな れんしゅう
Hiragana renshuu

1 Using the pictures of places, complete the sentences.

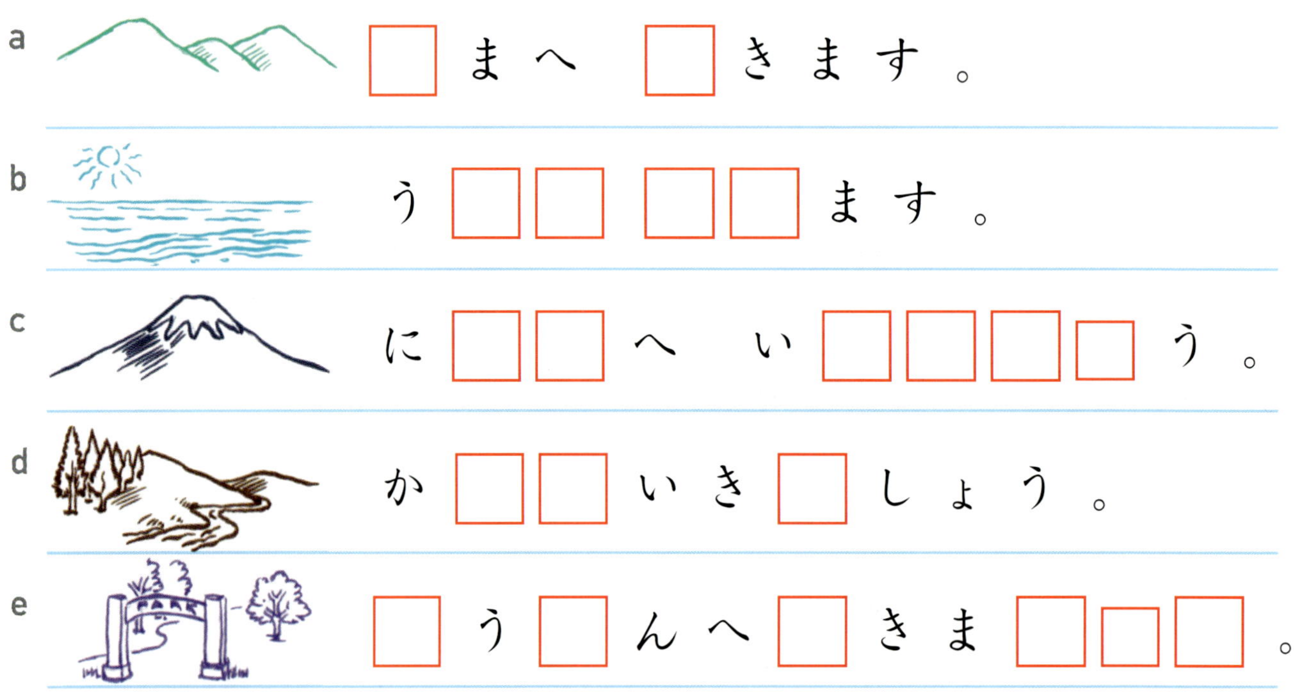

a □まへ □きます。

b う□□ □□ます。

c に□□へ い□□□□う。

d か□□いき□しょう。

e □う□んへ□きま□□□。

2 Using the pictures of people, complete the sentences.

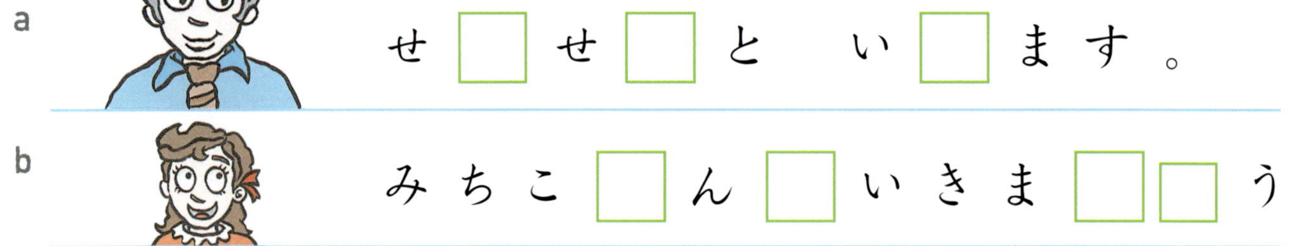

a せ□せ□と い□ます。

b みちこ□ん□いきま□□う。

3 Using the pictures of activities, write *Let's* …

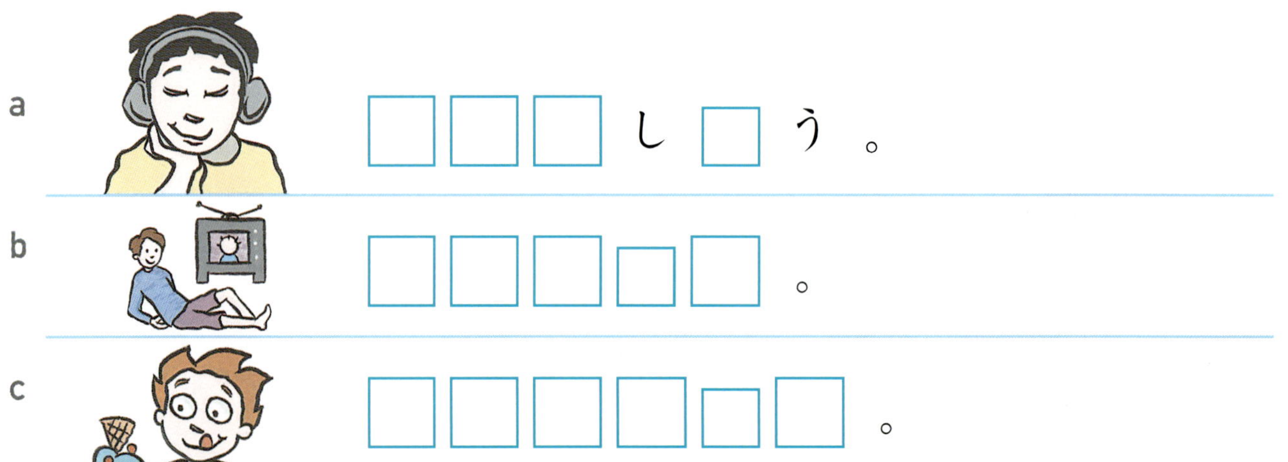

a □□□し□う。

b □□□□□。

c □□□□□□。

4 Write the names of the following Japanese cities and islands in hiragana.

a Tōkyō

e Honshuu

b Kyōto

f Kyuushuu

c Nagoya

g Shikoku

d Oosaka

h Hokkaidō

5 Write the following words in hiragana.

a today

b study べ

c together い に

d a little っ

e junior high school う こ

f primary school が う

g senior high school う

h social studies い

てんせい

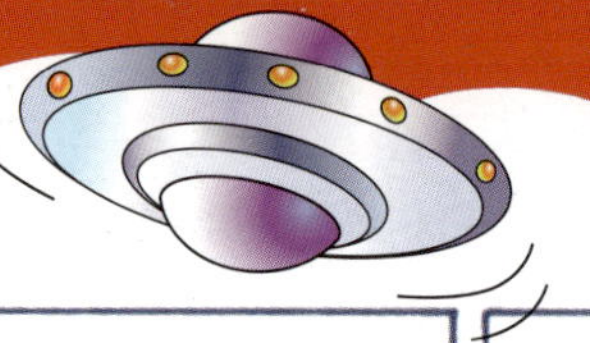

てんせいくん！
どこへ
いきますか？
SPORT

SPORT
やまへ
いきます。

だれと
いきますか。
ええっと…

いぬと
いきます。
SPORT

まって　ください！
いっしょに
いきましょうか？

いいえ!!

てんせいくんは　どこへ　いきますか。
いっしょに　いきましょう！

わあ！
わあ！
わあ！

AB pp. 72–73

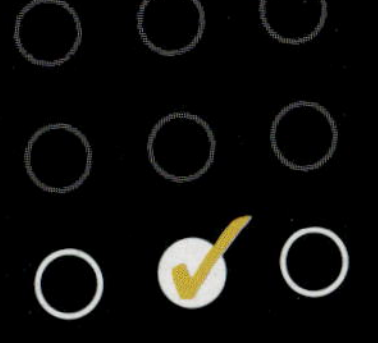

チェック しましょう
Chekku shimashō!

Verbs	
いきます	go
いきましょう	Let's go
ききましょう	Let's listen
しましょう	Let's do it
たべましょう	Let's eat
みましょう	Let's watch

Suffixes	
〜たち	plural ending

Adverb	
いっしょ (に)	together

Question words	
だれ	who

Expressions	
そうしましょう	Let's do that
ごめんなさい	Sorry

Food	
やきとり	grilled chicken
ポップコーン poppukoon	popcorn

Nouns	
えいが	movies
キャンプ kyanpu	camp
コーラス koorasu	choir
サーフィン saafin	surfing
つり	fishing
デート deeto	date
ぶんかさい	open day

Places			
アデレード Adereedo	Adelaide	シドニー Shidonii	Sydney
うみ	sea	にほん	Japan
オーストラリア Oosutoraria	Australia	パース Paasu	Perth
おばけやしき	haunted house	ブリスベン Burisuben	Brisbane
かわ	river	ホバート Hobaato	Hobart
キャンベラ Kyanbera	Canberra	まち	town
ケアンズ Keanzu	Cairns	メルボルン Meruboru n	Melbourne
こうえん	park	やま	mountain(s)

I can:

- ask where someone is going
- say where I am going
- ask who is going with someone
- say who is going with me
- invite someone to go with me
- invite someone to do four more things
- make the plural of ぼく and わたし
- say the names of seven Australian cities in Japanese
- read and write most things I can say using hiragana.

9
Unit

ひこうきで いきましょう!

Hikōki de ikimashō!

Let's go by plane!

1
だれ ですか。
えりかさん です。にほんの ポップ スター です。
poppu staa
うわあ、きれい ですね。

2
ぼくの いとこ です。
いとこ?

3
はい。えりかさんは きのう オーストラリアに きました。
Oosutoraria

4
どようびは えりかさんの パーティー です。
paatii
みなさん、うちに きて ください。
パーティー?
paatii
どようびに?
うわあ!

5
たのしい!
すごい!

6
わたしは すいようびに にほんへ かえります。みなさん、いっしょに きて ください。

7
でも、ちょっと たかい です。

8
わたしの ひこうきで いきましょう。

9
えりかさんの ひこうきで? すごい!

9
Sunshine City へ　いきましょう。
なんで いきましょうか。
10
あるいて　いきましょう。
うわあ、とうきょうは おおきい　ですね。
11
つぎは、あさくさへ　いきましょう。おみやげを　かいましょう。
なんで いきましょうか。
でんしゃで。
12
おもしろい　ですね。
きれい　ですね。
13
じゃ、てんぷらを たべましょうか おいしい　ですよ。
はい、てんぷらを たべましょう。
14
タクシーで　いきましょう。 Takushii
15
TAXI
THUMP!
いたい！

できますか
Dekimasuka
CAN YOU DO IT?

Can you find the expressions meaning …

- ✱ How shall we get there?
- ✱ on Saturday
- ✱ on foot
- ✱ by train
- ✱ by my plane.

せつめい コーナー
Setsumei koonaa

Explanation corner

How do I say what I have done?

To say what you have done, or did in the past, change the end of the verb from ます **masu** to ました **mashita**. For example: えりかさんは きのう きました。**Erika-san wa kinō kimashita.** (*Erika came yesterday.*)

To ask what someone did yesterday say, きのう、なにを しましたか。**Kinō, nani o shimashitaka.**

The verb in the answer will also end with ました。きのう、おんがくを ききました。**Kinō ongaku o kikimashita.** (*Yesterday I listened to music.*)

Of course, you can use other time words such as きょう **kyō** or the days of the week, which you will learn soon.

How do I talk about transport?

To ask what transport to use say, なんで いきますか。**Nan de ikimasuka.** (*How shall we go?*)

To answer that you will go by bus say, バスで いきます。**Basu de ikimasu.**

Notice that in the answer you replace the word なんで, which means *using what transport*, with the kind of transport + で.

Of course, if you are talking about what happened in the past, you would change いきます **ikimasu** to いきました **ikimashita.**

By the way, if you go on foot you say, あるいて いきます **aruite ikimasu.** あるいて means *walking*.

WHAT A USEFUL EXPRESSION!

うわあ！すごい！
Uwaa! Sugoi!

Use this to express admiration.

It's a bit like *Wow! Cool!*

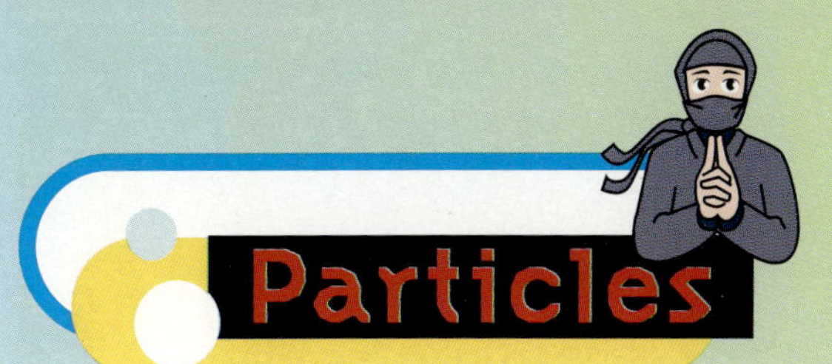
Particles

ひこうきで　いきましょ
Hikōki de ikimashō!

When the particle で follows transport it means *by* as in by bus, by car, by boat. Basically, it means *using* a.

Transport
で
Verb of movement
Go, come

Asking what someone did yesterday

Saying what you did yesterday

きのう、なにを　しましたか。
まちへ　いきました。
おみやげを　かいました。
てんぷらを
たべました。
おんがくを　ききました。
すいえいを　しました。

Asking what transport someone will use (used)

Saying what transport you use (used)

なんで　いきますか。
くるまで　いきます。
でんしゃで　いきます。
あるいて　いきます。

なんで がっこうへ いきますか

Nan de gakkō e ikimasuka

でんしゃで　いきます。
おそい、おそい！
タクシーで　いきます。
takushii
じてんしゃで
いきます。
バス
バスで　いきます。
basu
フェリーで
ferii
いきます。
くるまで
いきます。
あるいて
いきます。
みなさん
なんで
がっこうへ
いきますか。

AB pp. 74–75

できますか Dekimasuka CAN YOU DO IT?

1 Keiko and Akira are deciding what to do tomorrow. You are invited too. Listen to the passage and write down:

* where you are going
* how you will get there
* what time you will meet
* what you will do.

2 Naomi had a busy day in the city yesterday. She used lots of different means of transport. Listen to the passage and put numbers in the boxes to show the order in which she used them.

☐  ☐  ☐ 

☐  ☐  ☐ 
TAXI

3 Take turns. Kitsune did something yesterday. Kitsune secretly chooses a destination from box 1, a means of transport from box 2 and an activity from box 3. Tanuki must find out what Kitsune did and how by asking questions. Kitsune can only answer はい or いいえ. *For example:*

Tanuki: きのう、まちに　きましたか。 Kitsune: はい。
Tanuki: おみやげを　かいましたか。 Kitsune: いいえ。

mountains
park
river
sea
town
school
city
1

plane
on foot
bus
car
bicycle
train
taxi
2

swam
ate something
watched a movie
bought something
went jogging/fishing/camping
played tennis/football
3

3 Word puzzle

Find the Japanese words for the following English words in the puzzle. The words can go in any direction, including diagonally.

car	bus	to go	swimming	yes	movies	to begin
to play	to sleep	to study	plane	book	home	open day
train	on foot	bicycle	to eat	dinner	then	what time?
to listen	taxi	friend	no	where	who	
dog	to watch	to do	to get up	usually	together	

The leftover hiragana can be used to say *Where shall we go?* in Japanese.

で	ん	し	ゃ	あ	る	い	て	あ	そ	び	ま	す
き	バ	し	ま	す	は	い	き	ひ	こ	う	き	ど
き	ス	こ	う	ち	へ	ね	い	ま	た	べ	ま	す
ま	タ	ク	シ	ー	ほ	ん	ま	さ	す	い	い	え
す	じ	て	ん	し	ゃ	み	ま	す	な	ん	じ	は
く	る	ま	ど	こ	ま	い	っ	し	ょ	に	ぶ	じ
す	そ	し	て	し	え	い	ち	だ	も	と	ん	ま
い	お	き	ま	す	い	ょ	ぬ	だ	れ	う	か	り
え	た	い	て	い	が	ば	ん	ご	は	ん	さ	ま
い	べ	ん	き	ょ	う	し	ま	す	か	。	い	す

わかった！ Wakatta! I'VE GOT IT!

	[Optional]			
Asking what transport someone will use (used)	[Time word]	なんで	いきますか。(いきましたか。)	
Saying what transport you will use (used)	[Time word]	[transport] で	いきます。(いきました。)	
Asking what someone did	[Time word]	なにを	しましたか。	
Saying what you did	[Time word]	[place] へ	いきました。	I went to …
		[thing] を	たべました。	I ate a …
			みました。	I saw a …
			ききました。	I heard a …
			しました。	I did …
			べんきょう しました。	I studied …

あそびましょう Asobimashō!

Origami: making a talking Kitsune

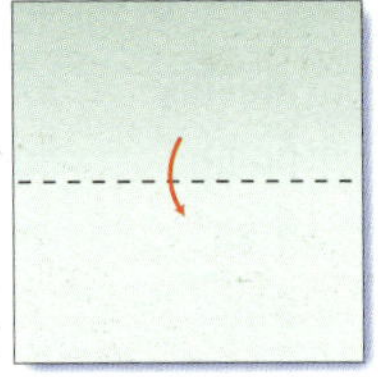

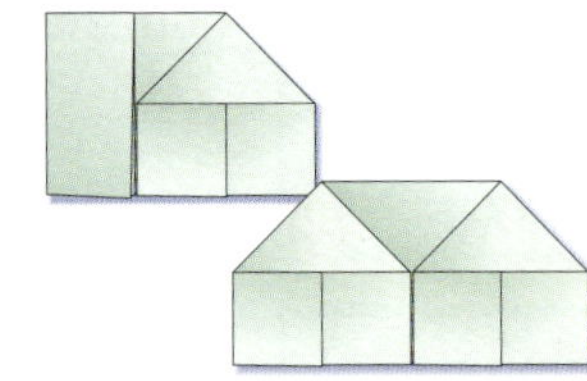

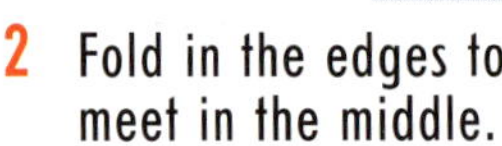

1 Fold in half.

2 Fold in the edges to meet in the middle.

3 Open and squash one flap.

4 Repeat with the other flap.

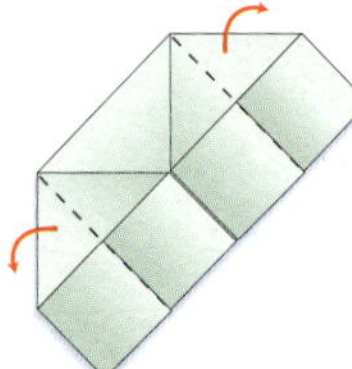

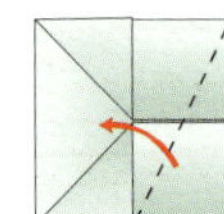

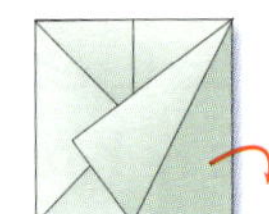

5 Fold into the back.

6 Fold diagonally.

7 Fold the same way on the other side.

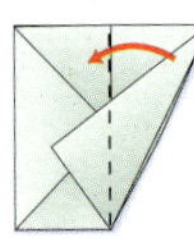

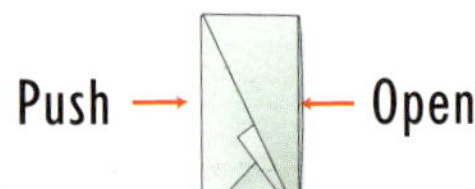
Push
Open

8 Fold the triangle part out.

9 Open while pushing the middle part in.

10 Draw eyes and whiskers.

11 Put your fingers in and it will talk!

インフォ

Info

DID YOU KNOW?

Japan's railway system

At the beginning of the Meiji era (1867), the Japanese government authorised the construction of a vast network of railways focused on Tōkyō. Since then, the railway system has developed into one of the most efficient in the world with fast, clean, punctual trains connecting the whole of Japan. Under the cities, networks of subways carry millions of people daily. Some of these trains have had the seats removed so that more people can fit in.

12
JR

Some trains are unique. The Shinkansen or bullet trains have been carrying passengers for more than thirty years at speeds of up to 225 km per hour. The most recent trains on this service can travel at over 250 km per hour and look like wingless jet planes! A high-speed magnetic levitation train (Maglev), which has run at 517 km per hour, is being developed and tested on a forty-three-kilometre test track to the west of Tōkyō. Eventually the track will be extended to run between Tōkyō and Oosaka.

Japan Rail's Twilight Express, a long-distance train that runs through western Japan, is luxuriously equipped to pamper the traveller.

The major stations are gigantic. Tōkyō Station has ten platforms for local trains; ten for the Shinkansen; and ten subway platforms. The station extends three stories above ground and five stories below. The station area is connected to nearby department stores and other buildings through a complex network of passages lined with cafes, restaurants and shops. On rainy days there is no need to get wet—you can travel all over the city underground, do your shopping, have lunch, visit some of the many exhibitions in the department stores and never see a single raindrop!

AB pp. 76–77

インフォ
Info
DID YOU KNOW?

The days of the week

The names given to the days of the week are very old and based on what the ancient scholars considered to be the most important elements in the universe: the sun 日, the moon 月, fire 火, water 水, trees 木, gold 金 and earth 土. The planets Mars 火星(かせい), Mercury 水星(すいせい), Jupiter 木星(もくせい), Venus 金星(きんせい) and Saturn 土星(どせい) are also named after these elements.

Days of the week in kanji and hiragana		Meanings of kanji	How the kanji were formed
Monday	月ようび (げつ)	月 means moon	月
Tuesday	火ようび (か)	火 means fire	火
Wednesday	水ようび (すい)	水 means water	水
Thursday	木ようび (もく)	木 means tree	木
Friday	金ようび (きん)	金 means gold	金
Saturday	土ようび (ど)	土 means earth	土
Sunday	日ようび (にち)	日 means sun	日

QUIZ

1 Find out how the days of the week in English got their names.

2 What names did the Romans use for the days of the week?

せつめい コーナー
Explanation corner Setsumei koonaa

How do I say the days of the week?

Each of the days of the week ends with ようび **yōbi**. This means *day*. The days have names, just as they do in English.

I heard that Monday came from 'the moon's day' in English; well in Japanese げつようび **Getsuyōbi** also means moon's day. Sunday also came from 'the sun's day', didn't it? Well, にちようび **Nichiyōbi** also means the sun's day!

When you ask the day of the week, use the same pattern as when asking the time. You just say, for example, なん ようび ですか。**Nan yōbi desuka.**

To answer that it is Monday say, げつようび です。**Getsuyōbi desu.**

To ask on what day someone does something, you use particle に **ni,** just as you did with time.

For example, なん ようびに いきますか。**Nan yōbi ni ikimasuka.** (*On what day are you going?*)

One answer could be にちようびに いきます。**Nichiyōbi ni ikimasu.** (*I'm going on Sunday.*)

To ask what day of the week it was yesterday, change です to でした **deshita**, like this: きのうは なんようび でしたか **Kinō wa, nan yōbi deshitaka.** To say it was Sunday say, きのうは にちようび でした **Kinō wa, Nichiyōbi deshita.**

きょうは なんようび ですか
Kyō wa nan yōbi desuka

Asking what day of the week it is / Saying the day of the week

きょうは なんようび ですか。
きょうは にちようび です。

Asking what day of the week it was / Saying what day of the week it was

きのうは なんようび でしたか。
THURSDAY NAOMI'S BIRTHDAY
きのうは もくようび でした。

Asking what day of the week someone goes somewhere / Answering

なんようびに うみに いきますか。
どようびに いきます。

Asking what day of the week someone did something / Answering

なんようびに えいがを みましたか。
かようびに みました。

AB p. 78

できますか
Dekimasuka
CAN YOU DO IT?

1 Today is Saturday. Masashi and Michiko have just arrived at a resort with their families. They are looking at a brochure and deciding how they will spend the week. Listen to their discussion and write the number of the activity or activities they choose next to the correct day.

Welcome to Hideaway Resort

Activities available

1 Tennis
2 Canoeing
3 Camping
4 Swimming
5 Surfing
6 Bungee jumping
7 Movies
8 Karaoke

土ようび Saturday	日ようび Sunday	月ようび Monday	火ようび Tuesday
水ようび Wednesday	木ようび Thursday	金ようび Friday	

2 Take turns. Kitsune makes the first half of a sentence. Tanuki must finish the sentence with a suitable ending using the past tense. Score one point for a suitable ending. Try to trick each other! *For example:*

Kitsune: げつようびに　てんぷらを ...
Tanuki: たべました。(1 point) or Tanuki: いきました。(no point)

You can use the following vocabulary, but why not find your own?

げつようび	やきとり (を)	いきました	かいました
かようび	えいが (を)	ききました	たべました
すいようび	いぬ (と)	みました	よみました
もくようび	おんがく (を)	あそびました	しました
きんようび	すいえい (を)		
どようび	こうえん (へ)		
にちようび			

ゲーム

Tanuki ninja and Kitsune ninja are trying to beat each other to the treasure in the ninja house. They must say the password and then move through the corridors. The password is a sentence that must start with the word they encounter. For example: くるまで　いきます or きのう　いきました. Take turns to move forward. Whoever makes a mistake must go back to the beginning, so listen carefully to what your partner is saying!

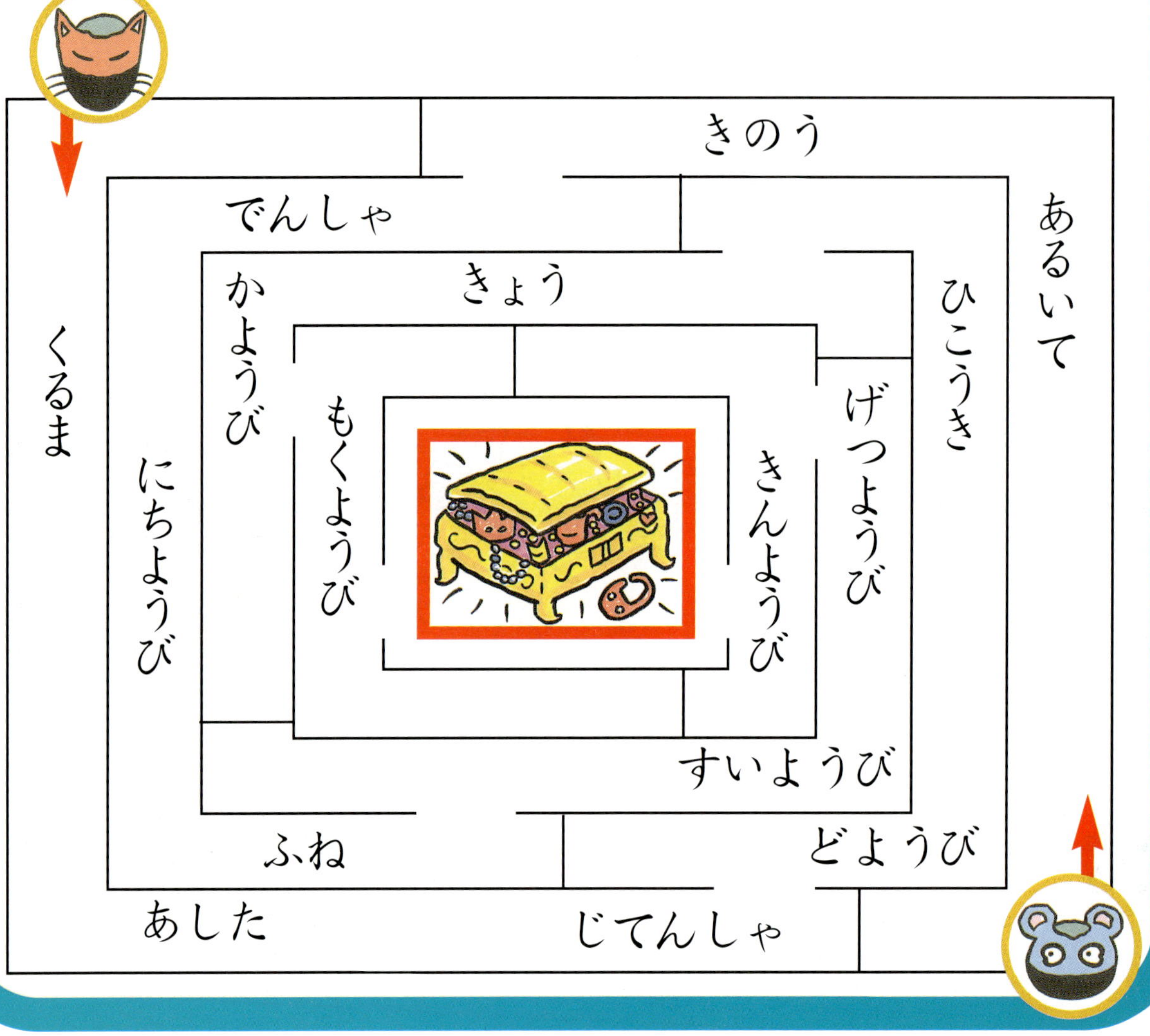

きのう
でんしゃ
あるいて
きょう
かようび
ひこうき
くるま
もくようび
げつようび
にちようび
きんようび
すいようび
ふね
どようび
あした
じてんしゃ

Hiragana puzzles

1 Put in the particles.

a なん＿いきますか。

b どこ＿いきますか。

c だれ＿いきますか。

d 6じ＿いきます。

e にちようび＿いきます。

2 Unscramble the words.

a えんこう

b しょいっに

c うのき

d したあ

e うきょ

f てあいる

3 Draw pictures of these forms of transport.

a ひこうき

b じてんしゃ

c でんしゃ

d くるま

e あるいて

わかった！ Wakatta! I'VE GOT IT!

Asking the days of the week	きょうは きのうは	なん	ようび	です でした	か。 か。
Saying the days of the week	げつ か すい もく きん ど にち	ようび	です。 でした。		
Asking on what day	なん	ようび	に	[action]	か。
Saying on what day	[Day's name]	ようび	に	[action]	

うたいましょう

Utaimashō

ようび の うた

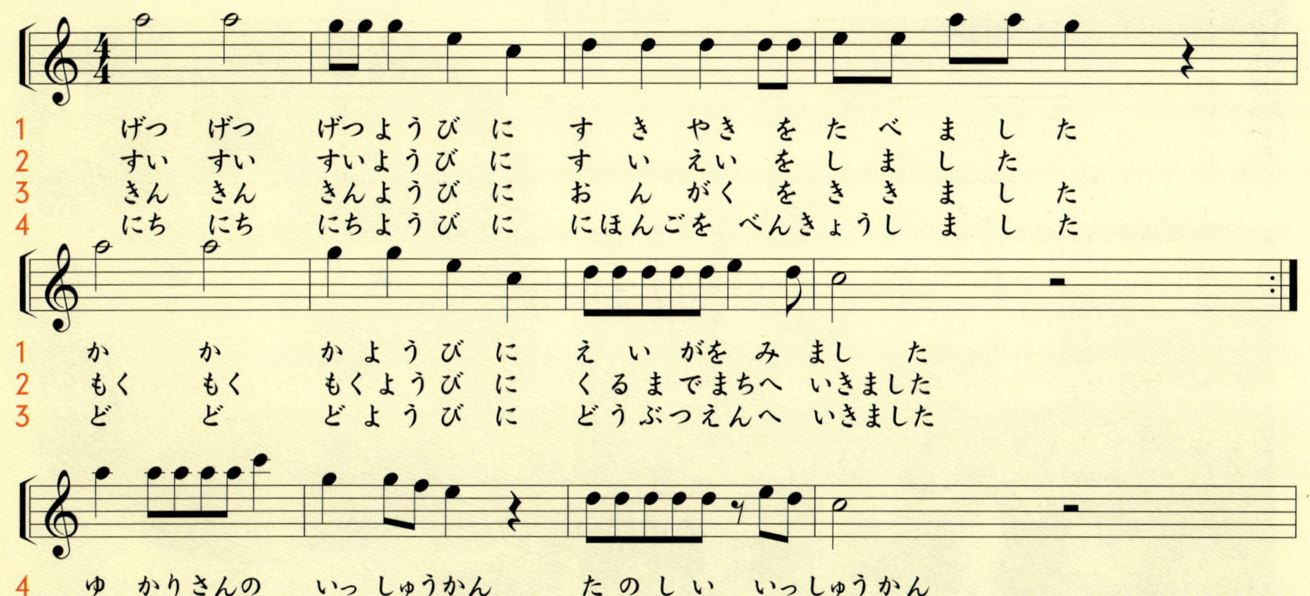
1 げつ げつ げつようびに すき やき をたべ まし た
2 すい すい すいようびに すい えい をしま し た
3 きん きん きんようびに おん がく をきき まし た
4 にち にち にちようびに にほんごを べんきょうし まし た
1 か か かようびに えいがを み まし た
2 もく もく もくようびに くるまでまちへ いきました
3 ど ど どようびに どうぶつえんへ いきました
4 ゆ かりさんの いっしゅうかん たのしい いっしゅうかん

なに？ なに？

Nani? Nani?

にちようびに　まちへ　いきました。
すいえいを　しました。
すいえいは　たのしい　ですよ。

どようびも　がっこうに
いきます。ぶんかさい
ですよ。ぶんかさいは
おもしろい　ですよ。

わたしたちは　おみやげを
かいます。おみやげは
たかい　ですね。

ぼくは　あるいて
まちに　いきます。

バーゲンコーナー
2F
ムセン
マイコン
Sale

AB pp. 79-80

ひらがな れんしゅう

Hiragana renshuu

Complete the following letter to a new penfriend by filling in the short blank spaces with the missing hiragana and place your personal details on the long lines.

こん____ ____は。わ____ ____ or ぼ____は__________

____す。どうぞ____ ____ ____ ____。__________じん

で____。__________に す____ ____います。でん____

____んごうは__________です。____さい____ ____。

____ねん____ ____です。す____な たべ____ ____は

__________です。__________も お____し____です。

わ____し or ぼ____の がっ____ ____は おも____ ____ ____

です。すき____か____ ____は__________です。

__________も たの____ ____です。えい____の

せん____ ____は__________です。

____たし or ぼく____たい____い____じに おき____ ____。

それから、____じ____あさ____ ____ ____を た____ま____。

がっ____ ____は ____じに はじ____ります。

わ____し or ぼ____は________で (or ある____ ____)

が____こう____いき____す。

どよう____に た____てい__________を します。

____ようび____ __________を____ます。

さよ____ ____ ____。

____

てんせい

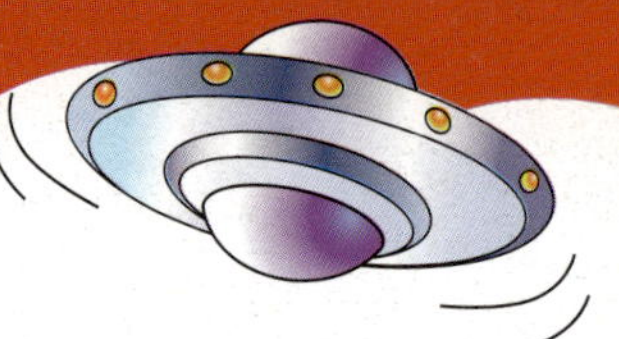

てんせいくん …

てんせいくんは
なんようびに
かえりますか。

ええっと … てんせいくんは …
もくようびに
うちゅうへ
いきましたね。

きょうは　にちようび
ですね！

てんせいくん！てんせいくん！

あ！てんせいくんと …

わあ …

てんせいくん
いぬは？
いぬ？ええっと … あのう、
いぬこさん　です。
どうぞ
よろしく！

ただいま！
てんせいくん
おかえりなさい！

あ !!

いぬこです。
どうぞ　よろしく。

AB pp. 81–82

チェックしましょう！
Chekku shimashō!

Time words	
きのう	yesterday
げつようび	Monday
かようび	Tuesday
すいようび	Wednesday
もくようび	Thursday
きんようび	Friday
どようび	Saturday
にちようび	Sunday

Adjectives	
いたい	it hurts/Ouch!
おおきい	big
きれい	pretty, clean
すごい	terrific, cool
たかい	expensive, high

Question words	
なんで	by what means?
なんようび	what day?

Other nouns	
いとこ	cousin
うち	home
おみやげ	souvenir, gift
パーティー paatii	party

Verbs	
あるいて	walking
いきました	went
かいます	buy
かえります	return, come back
きて ください	please come
きました	came

Expressions	
おかえりなさい	Welcome home
ただいま	I'm home

Transport	
くるま	car
じてんしゃ	bicycle
タクシー takushii	taxi
でんしゃ	train
バス basu	bus
ひこうき	plane
フェリー ferii	ferry

I can:

- ask what someone did yesterday
- say six things that I did yesterday
- ask what transport someone will use or used
- say what transport I will use or used
- say all the days of the week
- ask what day someone will do or did something
- say what day someone will do or did something
- say what day I will do or did something
- read and write everything I can say using hiragana.

Vocabulary list

English–Japanese

A

a bit ちょっと
Adelaide アデレード (Adereedo)
American person アメリカじん (Amerika-jin)
art びじゅつ
Australia オーストラリア (Oosutoraria)
Australian person オーストラリアじん (Oosutoraria-jin)

B

bag かばん
begins はじまります
begin はじめます
bicycle じてんしゃ
big おおきい
blackboard こくばん
book ほん
boring つまらない
breakfast あさごはん
Brisbane ブリスベン (Burisuben)
brush ふで
bus バス (basu)
but でも
by what means なんで

C

Cairns ケアンズ (Keanzu)
calligraphy ink すみ
came きました
camp キャンプ (kyampu)
Canadian person カナダじん (Kanada-jin)
Canberra キャンベラ (Kyanbera)
car くるま
chair いす
Chinese person ちゅうごくじん
choir コーラス (koorasu)
class, Class ~ くみ、〜ぐみ
clean きれい
coloured pencils いろえんぴつ
come back かえります
Cool! / Terrific! すごい！

D

delicious おいしい
design and technology ぎじゅつかてい
desk つくえ
difficult むずかしい
dinner ばんごはん
do します
dog いぬ
door ドア (doa)

E

earlier もっとはやい
early はやい
easy やさしい
eat たべます
eight はち（八）
eleven じゅういち（十一）
English えいご
entertaining おもしろい
eraser けしゴム (keshigomu)
everyone みなさん
Excuse me すみません
expensive たかい

F

favourite	すきな
five	ご（五）
food	たべもの
forest	もり（森）
four	し、よん、よ（四）
Friday	きんようび（金曜日）
friend	ともだち
fun	たのしい

G

game, contest	しあい
game	ゲーム (geemu)
gentle	やさしい
geography	ちり
German person	ドイツじん (Doitsu-jin)
get up	おきます
ghost house	おばけやしき
glue	のり
go	いきます
go to bed, sleep	ねます
Good afternoon	こんにちは
Good evening	こんばんは
Good morning	おはよう（ございます）
Good night	おやすみなさい
Goodbye (see you)	じゃ、また
Goodbye (return safely)	いってらっしゃい
Goodbye (I'm off)	いってきます
Goodbye	さようなら
grade in school	〜ねんせい
grilled chicken	やきとり

H

half	はん
hamburger	ハンバーガー (hanbaagaa)
hat	ぼうし
Hello	こんにちは
Hello (I'm home)	ただいま
Hello (on the phone)	もしもし
Hi	おはよう、こんにちは
high	たかい
high school	こうこう
history	れきし
Hobart	ホバート (Hobaato)
home	うち
hot	あつい
hot dog	ホットドッグ (hottodoggu)
hour	じ
hurts	いたい

I

I'm home	ただいま
I've done it	できました
I (boy speaking)	ぼく
I (girl speaking)	わたし
Indonesian person	インドネシアじん (Indoneshia-jin)
interesting	おもしろい
is, am	です

J

Japan	にほん（日本）
Japanese language	にほんご、こくご
Japanese person	にほんじん
jogging	ジョギング (jogingu)
joke	じょうだん
junior high school	ちゅうがっこう

K

kind	しんせつ
kindergarten	ようちえん

L

lasagna	ラザーニャ (razaanya)
late	おそい
later	もっとおそい
Let me see ...	ええっと ...
Let's do it	しましょう
Let's do that	そう しましょう
Let's eat	たべましょう

Let's go	いきましょう
Let's listen	ききましょう
Let's watch	みましょう
listen	ききます
live, am living	すんで います。
look at	みます
lunch	ひるごはん

M

make a phone call	でんわを します
map	ちず
match, game	しあい
maths	すうがく
may I close	しめても いい ですか
may I eat	たべても いい ですか
may I go	いっても いい ですか
may I listen	きいても いい ですか
may I open	あけても いい ですか
may I read	よんでも いい ですか
may I see	みても いい ですか
may I sit	すわっても いい ですか
may I stand	たっても いい ですか
may I take	とっても いい ですか
may I write	かいても いい ですか
meat pie	ミートパイ (miitopai)
minute	ふん、ぷん
Miss ~	~ さん
Mister, master ~	~ くん
Monday	げつようび（月曜日）
moon	つき（月）
mountains	やま（山）
movies	えいが
music	おんがく
my (boy speaking)	ぼくの
my (girl speaking)	わたしの

N

New Zealander	ニュージーランドじん (Nyuujiirando-jin)
nine	きゅう、く（九）
no	いいえ
No, you may not	いいえ だめです
notebook	ノート (nooto)
now	いま
number suffix	~ ばんごう

O

o'clock	~ じ
on foot	あるいて
once more	もう いちど
one	いち（一）
open day	ぶんかさい
Ouch!	いたい

P

packed lunch	おべんとう
paper	かみ
park	こうえん
party	パーティー (paatii)
pencil case	ふでばこ
pencils	えんぴつ
period	じかん
person	~ じん
Perth	パース (Paasu)
phone	でんわ
phone number	でんわ ばんごう
phys. ed.	たいいく
pizza	ピザ (piza)
plane	ひこうき
play, have fun	あそびます
please	どうぞ
please close	しめて ください
please come	きて ください
please get up	おきて ください
please go to bed	ねて ください
please lend me	かして ください
please listen	きいて ください
please look	みて ください
please open	あけて ください
please read	よんで ください
please say	いって ください
please show	みせて ください

please sit　すわって　ください
please stand　たって　ください
please take　とって　ください
please wait　まって　ください
please write　かいて　ください
Pleased to meet you　どうぞよろしく
popcorn　ポップコーン (poppukoon)
pretty　きれい
primary school　しょうがっこう

Q

quietly　しずかに

R

Really? Is that so?　そう　ですか
return　かえります
river　かわ（川）
rose　ばら

S

salty　からい
sandwich(es)　サンドイッチ (sandoitchi)
Saturday　どようび（土曜日）
school　がっこう
science　りか
scissors　はさみ
sea　うみ
See you again　じゃ、また
See you tomorrow　じゃ、また　あした
senior high school　こうこう
seven　しち、なな（七）
six　ろく（六）
skateboard　スケートボード (sukeetoboodo)
so so　まあまあ
social studies　しゃかい
Sorry　ごめんなさい、すみません
souvenir　おみやげ
spaghetti　スパゲッティ (supagetti)
spicy　からい
strict　きびしい
study　べんきょう　します
subject　かもく
Sunday　にちようび（日曜日）
surname　みょうじ
sweet　あまい
swim　すいえいを　します
Sydney　シドニー (Shidonii)

T

taxi　タクシー (takushii)
teacher　せんせい
ten　じゅう（十）
tennis　テニス (tenisu)
Terrific!　すごい
Thank you　ありがとう
That's right　そう　です
then　そして
three　さん（三）
Thursday　もくようび（木曜日）
timetable　じかんわり
today　きょう
together　いっしょに
tomorrow　あした
train　でんしゃ
training　トレーニング (toreeningu)
Try hard!　がんばって！
Tuesday　かようび（火曜日）
TV　テレビ (terebi)
twelve　じゅうに（十二）
twenty　はたち、にじゅう（二十）
two　に（二）

U

Um, excuse me ...　あのう ...
unpleasant taste　まずい
usually　たいてい

V

very much, really　どうも

W

walking	あるいて
watch	みます
Wednesday	すいようび（水曜日）
Welcome home	おかえりなさい
Well done!	よく できました！
well then	あのう
went	いきました
what	なん
what age	なん さい
what day	なん ようび
what number	なん ばん
what time	なん じ
where	どこ
who	だれ
window	まど
Wow!	うわあ

Y

years old	~ さい
yes	はい
Yes, that's fine	はい、いいです
You're welcome	どういたしまして

Japanese–English

あ

あけて　ください	please open
あさごはん	breakfast
あした	tomorrow
あそびます	to play
あつい	hot
アデレード (Adereedo)	Adelaide
あのう …	Um, excuse me …
あまい	sweet
アメリカじん (Amerika-jin)	American person
ありがとう	Thank you
あるいて	walking

い

いいえ	no
いいえ、だめです	No, you may not
いきました	went
いきましょう	Let's go
いきます	to go
いす	chair
いたい！	Ouch!
いち（一）	one
いっしょに	together
いってきます	Goodbye (I'm off)
いって　ください	please say
いってらっしゃい	Goodbye (return safely)
いぬ	dog
いま	now
いろえんぴつ	coloured pencils
インドネシアじん (Indoneshia-jin)	Indonesian person

う

うみ	sea
うわあ！	Wow!

え

えいが	movies
えいご	English
ええっと …	Let me see …
えんぴつ	pencils

お

おいしい	delicious
おおきい	big
オーストラリア (Oosutoraria)	Australia
オーストラリアじん (Oosutoraria-jin)	Australian person
おかえりなさい	Welcome home
おきて　ください	please get up
おきます	to get up
おくに	your country
おそい	late
おなまえ	your name
おばけやしき	ghost house
おはよう（ございます）	Good morning
おべんとう	packed lunch
おもしろい	interesting, entertaining
おやすみなさい	Good night
おんがく	music

か

かい	shell
かいて　ください	please write
かえりました	came back
かえります	to come back
かして　ください	please lend me
がっこう	school
カナダじん (Kanada-jin)	Canadian person
かばん	bag
かみ	paper
かもく	subjects
からい	salty, spicy
カレーライス (kareeraisu)	curry and rice
かようび（火曜日）	Tuesday
かわ	river
がんばって！	Try hard!

き

きいて　ください	please listen
ききましょう	Let's listen
ききます	to listen, hear

ぎじゅつかてい	design and technology
きて　ください	please come
きのう	yesterday
きびしい	strict
きました	came
きれい	pretty, clean
キャンプ (kyanpu)	camp
キャンベラ (Kyanbera)	Canberra
きゅう、く（九）	nine
きょう	today
きんようび（金曜日）	Friday

く

く、きゅう（九）	nine
くみ、～ぐみ	class, Class ~
くるま	car
～くん	Mister ~, Master ~

け

ケアンズ (keanzu)	Cairns
ゲーム (geemu)	game
けしゴム (gomu)	eraser
げつようび（月曜日）	Monday

こ

ご（五）	five
こうえん	park
こうこう	senior high school
コーラス (koorasu)	choir
こくご	Japanese
こくばん	blackboard
ごめんなさい	Sorry
こんにちは	Good afternoon, Hello
こんばんは	Good evening

さ

～さい	~ years old
さようなら	Goodbye
さん（三）	three
～さん	Miss, Mrs, Ms, Mr ~
サンドイッチ (sandoitchi)	sandwich(es)

し

し、よ、よん（四）	four
～じ	~ o'clock
しあい	match, game
じかん	time, hour
じかんわり	timetable
しずかに	quietly
しち、なな（七）	seven
じてんしゃ	bicycle
シドニー (Shidonii)	Sydney
しましょう	Let's do it
します	to do
しめて　ください	please close
しゃかい	social studies
じゃ、また	See you again
じゃ、また　あした	See you tomorrow
じゅう（十）	ten
じゅういち（十一）	eleven
じゅうに（十二）	twelve
しょうがっこう	primary school
じょうぎ	ruler
じょうだん	joke
ジョギング (jogingu)	jogging
～じん	~ person
しんせつ	kind

す

すいえいを　します	to swim
すいようび（水曜日）	Wednesday
すうがく	maths
すきな	favourite
スケートボード (sukeetoboodo)	skateboard
すごい！	Terrific!, Cool!
スパゲッティ (supagetti)	spaghetti
すみ	calligraphy ink
すみません	Excuse me, Sorry

すわって ください | please sit
すんで います | to live

せ

せんせい | teacher

そ

そう しましょう | Let's do that
そう です | That's right
そう ですか | Really? Is that so?
そして | then

た

たいいく | phys. ed.
たいてい | usually
たかい | high, expensive
タクシー (takushii) | taxi
ただいま | I'm home
たって ください | please stand
たのしい | fun
たべましょう | Let's eat
たべます | to eat
たべもの | food
だれ | who

ち

ちず | map
ちゅうがっこう | junior high school
ちゅうごくじん | Chinese person
ちょっと | a bit
ちり | geography

つ

つき（月） | moon
つくえ | desk
つまらない | boring

て

できました | I've done it
です | is, am
テニス (tenisu) | tennis
でも | but
テレビ (terebi) | TV
でんしゃ | train
でんわ | phone
でんわ ばんごう | phone number
でんわを します | to make a phone call

と

ドア (doa) | door
ドイツじん (Doitsu-jin) | German person
どういたしまして | You're welcome
どうぞ | please
どうぞ よろしく | Pleased to meet you
どうも | very much, really
どこ | where
ともだち | friends
トレーニング (toreeningu) | training

な

なな、しち（七） | seven
なん | what
なん さい | what age
なん じ | what time
なんで | by what means
なん ばん | what number
なん ようび | what day

に

に（二） | two
にじゅう（二十） | twenty
にちようび（日曜日） | Sunday
にほん（日本） | Japan
にほんご | Japanese language
にほんじん | Japanese person
ニュージーランドじん (Nyuujiirando-jin) | New Zealander

ね

ねて ください	please go to bed
ねます	to go to bed, sleep
~ ねんせい	grade ~ in school

の

ノート (nooto)	notebook
のり	glue

は

パース (Paasu)	Perth
パーティー (paatii)	party
はい	yes
はい、いいです	Yes, that's fine
はさみ	scissors
はじめます	to begin
バス (basu)	bus
はたち、にじゅう（二十）	twenty
はち（八）	eight
はやい	early
ばら	rose
はん	half
~ ばん	number suffix
ばんごう	number
ばんごはん	dinner
ハンバーガー (hanbaagaa)	hamburger

ひ

ひ（日）	sun
ひこうき	airplane
ピザ (piza)	pizza
びじゅつ	art
ひるごはん	lunch

ふ

ふで	brush
ふでばこ	pencil case
ブリスベン (Burisuben)	Brisbane
ふん、ぷん	minute
ぶんかさい	open day

へ

べんきょうします	to study

ほ

ぼうし	hat, cap
ぼく	I (boy speaking)
ぼくの	my (boy speaking)
ホットドッグ (hottodoggu)	hot dog
ポップコーン (poppukoon)	popcorn
ホバート (Hobaato)	Hobart
ほん	book

ま

まあまあ	so so
まずい	unpleasant taste
まって ください	please wait
まど	window

み

ミートパイ (miitopai)	meat pie
みせて ください	please show me
みて ください	please look
みなさん	everyone
みましょう	Let's watch
みます	to look at, watch
みょうじ	surname

む

むずかしい	difficult

も

もう	already

もう いちど	once more
もくようび（木曜日）	Thursday
もしもし	Hello (on the phone)
もっと おそい	later
もっと はやい	earlier

や

やきとり	grilled chicken
やさしい	easy
やま（山）	mountains

よ

よ、よん、し（四）	four
ようちえん	kindergarten
よく できました！	Well done!
よんで ください	please read

ら

ラザーニャ (razaanya)	lasagna

り

りか	science

れ

れきし	history

ろ

ろく（六）	six

わ

わたし	I (girl speaking)
わたしの	my (girl speaking)